D0065026

WITHDRAWN

A Life with Karol

A Life with Karol

My Forty-Year Friendship with the Man Who Became Pope

CARDINAL STANISLAW DZIWISZ

in Conversation with Gian Franco Svidercoschi

TRANSLATED FROM THE ITALIAN BY
ADRIAN J. WALKER

DOUBLEDAY
NEW YORK LONDON TORONTO SYDNEY AUCKLAND

LEWES PUBLIC LIBRARY, INC.
111 ADAMS AVENUE
LEWES, DE 19958
(302) 645-4633

PUBLISHED BY DOUBLEDAY

Published in the United States by Doubleday, an imprint of The Doubleday Broadway Publishing Group, a division of Random House, Inc., New York.
www.doubleday.com

DOUBLEDAY and the portrayal of an anchor with a dolphin are registered trademarks of Random House, Inc.

English translation copyright © 2008 by Doubleday

All Rights Reserved

Originally published in Italy as *Una Vita con Karol* by RCS Libri S.p.A., Milan. This edition published by arrangement with RCS Libri S.p.A., Milan.

Copyright © 2007 by Libreria Editrice Vaticana, Vatican City
Copyright © 2007 by RCS Libri S.p.A., Milan

Book design by Lovedog Studio

Frontispiece photograph: John Paul II ordaining Bishop Stanislaw Dziwisz, March 19, 1998. Courtesy *L'Osservatore Romano*;
© 1979 Libreria Editrice Vaticana

Library of Congress Cataloging-in-Publication Data
Dziwisz, Stanislaw.
[Vita con Karol. English]
A life with Karol : my forty-year friendship with the man who became pope / Stanislaw Dziwisz.—1st ed.
p. cm.
1. John Paul II, Pope, 1920–2005. 2. Dziwisz, Stanislaw—Interviews.
3. Bishops—Poland—Interviews. 4. Catholic Church—Clergy—Interviews.
I. Title.
BX1378.5.D9713 2007
282.092—dc22
[B]
2007022374

ISBN 978-0-385-52374-5

PRINTED IN THE UNITED STATES OF AMERICA

1   3   5   7   9   10   8   6   4   2

FIRST AMERICAN EDITION

Contents

Part One

The Polish Years

Part Two

The Papal Years

Farewell to a Beloved Face

It was the last time I would see him.

Oh, of course I was going to see him again a thousand other times after that—every hour of every day, in fact. I was going to see him again with the eyes of faith. And, of course, with the eyes of my heart and my memory. I was going to keep feeling his presence, too, though it would take a different form from the one I had been used to.

But this was the last time I would see his face—how shall I put it?—physically. Humanly. It was the last time I would see the man who had been a father and a teacher to me. The last time I would see his body, his hands, and, most important, his face. And his face reminded me of how he would look at you. In fact, that was always the first thing that struck you about him: his gaze.

And so I didn't want this moment to end. I did everything slowly, trying to stretch it into an eternity.

Until, all of a sudden, I felt a pair of eyes staring at me. And then I realized what I had to do.

I took the white veil and laid it gently over his face. I was almost afraid of hurting him, as if that piece of silk could actually bother or annoy him.

I found strength in the prayer of the veiling ceremony: "Lord and Father, may he now behold You face-to-face; having departed this life, may his face contemplate Your beauty."

He was at home with the Father now and could finally see Him face-to-face. His earthly adventure was over, and he had put in at port.

So I started attending to the words of the prayer myself. And as I was praying, I began to remember. I began to relive the forty years that I—an insignificant man almost accidentally touched by the "mystery"—had spent at Karol Wojtyla's side.

Narrator's Preface

The "Mystery"
of John Paul II

Of all images of Karol Wojtyla, the one that has stuck most vividly in my mind's eye and in my heart comes from his first papal visit to Poland, in June 1979, and, in particular, from his now-famous meeting with the university students.

It was morning. The Vistula was in the background and the sun was just barely up. Warsaw was bathed in an extraordinary atmosphere of calm. As soon as the Pope started speaking, the whole crowd was seized with excitement. And at the end of Wojtyla's speech, his thousands of young listeners, as if on cue, simultaneously raised their little wooden crosses toward him.

At the time, I grasped only the political implications of what was happening. I realized that things had changed, that the rising generations of Poles were by now inoculated against communism, and that before long Poland would be rocked by an earthquake.

But that sea of wooden crosses contained the seeds of something much greater than a popular revolution. They held a "mystery," which I wasn't completely aware of at the time. I saw this mystery again twenty-six years later in the endless throngs that came to say their last farewell to John Paul II. This second time, I knew what I was seeing.

These crowds revealed, I think, the profound meaning of Karol Wojtyla's legacy. He showed the face of God, God's human visage, if you will. He displayed the features of God incarnate. He thus became an interpreter and instrument of God's Father-hood, a man who narrowed the gap between heaven and earth, transcendence and immanence. And in so doing, he laid the groundwork for a new spirituality and a new way of living the faith in modern society.

So in the midst of that crowd in Warsaw, there was a mys-tery—a mystery at whose side Father Stanislaw Dziwisz spent forty years of his life. In what follows, we—he as witness and I as narrator—will attempt, if not to unveil the mystery, then at least to tell its story.

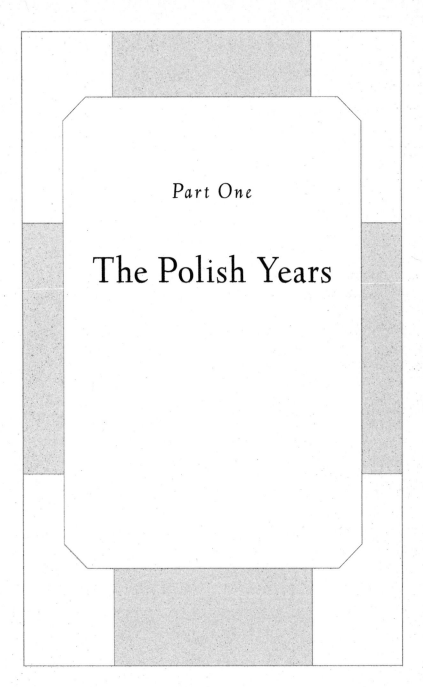

Part One

The Polish Years

1.

The First Meeting

It all began on an October day in 1966, which was the start of something like a new life for Stanislaw Dziwisz. Because it was on that day that he was asked by the archbishop of Kraków to become his personal secretary. Wojtyla had decided that the young priest would make an outstanding assistant, one whom he could entrust not only with the management of his appointment calendar but also with his confidences, his thoughts, and even— why not?—with a bit of his heart.

He looked right at me and said, "I'd like you to come live here . . . and give me a hand."

Stanislaw was born in 1939 in Raba Wyźna, a village in the foothills of the Tatras, Poland's principal mountain chain. So it was logical that he would learn to ski as a child and would become a connoisseur of snow and ski slopes. He was the fifth of seven children, five boys and two girls.

His father, Stanislaw Dziwisz, Sr., worked for the railroad. His mother, Zofia, took care of the household and the upbringing of *the kids. It was she who taught them what it means to live out Gospel charity. The doors of the Dziwisz home were always open to the poor and the needy. If you visited them in the evening, you could always be sure of a hot meal and a place to spend the night.*

But World War II was raging. The Germans had invaded Poland from the west and the Soviets had marched in from the east.

Those were terrible years for everybody, and we were no exception. There were so many mouths to feed, but it wasn't easy to find food. And on top of that, my family was hiding a Jewish man. That was dangerous, given the risk of detection. Who knows where we might all have ended up if the Nazis had found out.

Not too far away from us, in Rokiciny Podhalańskie, the Gestapo had arrested the superior of the Ursulines, Sister Maria Clemensa Staszewska, because she had given sanctuary to some Jewish women in the convent. Sadly, she ended up in Auschwitz.

The only thing we knew about the man hiding in our house was his name, Wilhelm. Actually, we kids called him "Wilus." He was from Wadowice. He had escaped from the Nazis, though how he ended up at our house was something of a mystery. He was a likable man. He stayed with us until the end of the war, and would do little odd jobs around the house to help out. He bid us all a tearful good-bye before he left. But we completely lost track of him after that.

After the end of the war, Poland began to breathe a little more easily, although storm clouds were glowering threateningly on the horizon. The "liberators" from the east did not seem particu-

larly interested in leaving. And at the Dziwisz home, there was a terrible tragedy.

It happened on a typical morning while my father was on his way to work. He was struck by a train as he was crossing the tracks. He was only thirty-nine. When they came to break the news to us, I immediately went totally cold, realizing I would never feel his hand on my shoulder again. My mother was a woman of great faith and courage. Despite the huge grief she was carrying in her heart, she showered us with love. And she managed to raise the seven of us, magically multiplying her modest pension.

Stanislaw was going on nine when his father died. He had to grow up in a hurry, but he did his part. After finishing elementary school, he started attending high school in Nowy Targ. Meanwhile, though, another vocation was budding inside him: He wanted to become a priest, a minister of God. So after graduation, he entered the seminary. It was 1957. And it was then that he first met Father Karol Wojtyla, who at that time was a professor of moral theology at the seminary.

He immediately made a big impression on me. First of all because he was so devout and learned, plus being an outstanding lecturer. But also because he had an easy way of relating to people. On one hand, my classmates and I felt that he moved in a higher sphere than we did because of his deep interior life and his amazing intellectual qualifications. On the other hand, it was obvious to us that he took a close interest in our lives, and we saw how easily he opened up to other people and entered into human relationships.

◆   ◆   ◆

The year 1956 inaugurated a time of major change in Eastern Europe. In February, Khrushchev used the XXth Congress of the Communist Party of the Soviet Union as a platform to denounce Stalin and condemn his grisly crimes. In June, there was a workers' revolt in Poznań, instigated by revisionist backers of Gomulka, the chief spokesman of a national way to communism. Cardinal Wyszynski was released after thirty-seven months of confinement, and other bishops were let out of prison, as well.

Admittedly, there were completely opposite signals, too, such as the Soviet tanks that bloodily suppressed the October uprising in Hungary. And yet, at least in Poland, there was more breathing room, even for the Church. In December 1956, Father Wojtyla was finally appointed to the chair of ethics at the Catholic University of Lublin, where he was already teaching. Despite his new position, he also continued teaching at the Kraków seminary.

I remember that in the third year he taught us the principia— that is, the fundamental philosophical principles of moral theology. Although those lectures were pretty hard for us, he prepared them extremely carefully. In fact, I'd have to say perfectly. It was in those lectures that we got the philosophical background we needed to go on with further studies in moral theology. But Father Wojtyla had a lot of responsibilities, and he was increasingly absorbed by them. He was only thirty-eight when he was named auxiliary bishop of Kraków. And being a bishop was something he took really seriously. By the time we entered the sixth year, he stopped teaching completely, because he no longer had the time to lecture at the seminary. The archbishop, Eugeniusz Baziak, had died, and Wojtyla became the capitulary vicar, which meant that he had to take over responsibility for the whole diocese.

The great day arrived. On June 23, 1963, Stanislaw received Holy Orders from his former moral theology professor. He had become a priest. Shortly afterward, he was sent as associate pastor to the parish of Maków Podhalański. It was one of the best parishes in the diocese: It was modern, well-managed, and had a lot of ministries—for example, for the sick, for children, and for families.

I'm really glad to talk about that, because it was an unforgettable experience. The pastor was an excellent priest by the name of Franciszek Dzwigonski. He had divided the parish community into several sectors and appointed someone in each sector to keep him informed about what was going on—for example, who was sick, who was having problems or was out of work, or if there were neglected children. Could there be a better apprenticeship for a young priest?

Two years went by, and then Father Dziwisz left the parish because his superiors wanted him to pursue further studies. He consulted the rector of the seminary about which field he should choose—patristics or Scripture. Finally, it turned out that there was need for a liturgist. He thus began to do the necessary research, first for the licentiate, then for the doctorate. The topic of his doctoral dissertation was the cult of Saint Stanislas in the diocese of Kraków up to the time of the Council of Trent. But, just twelve months into the project, Archbishop Wojtyla summoned him unexpectedly to the episcopal residence.

It was October 8, 1966, the day that would change Stanislaw Dziwisz's life forever. He was twenty-seven years old.

As soon as I came in to see him, he looked straight at me and said, "I'd like you to come live here. You can continue your studies and give me a hand." "When?" I asked. He replied, "Today will work." He turned toward the window and noticed that it was getting late. "Go to the chancellor and he'll show you the room." "I'll come tomorrow," I said. He watched me leave with a certain curiosity, but I noticed that he was smiling.

2.

New Men

So far, Stansilaw had only known Wojtyla a bit distantly and su-perficially as a professor and as a bishop. He had some sense of Wojtyla's personal history and his religious journey, but that was all. However, now that he was Wojtyla's secretary and was living with him in the spacious episcopal residence on Franciszkańska Street, Stanislaw got to know him well. He became familiar with the archbishop's pastoral ideas, his plans for the Church, and, above all, his profound spirituality, starting with how he cele-brated Mass.

He never started Mass without a period of *silentium* beforehand. If we were driving to some parish for a pastoral visit or some church to say Mass, he would never talk or waste time chatting in the car, but would always be immersed in meditation and prayer. Since it was his job to celebrate Mass and the like, he tried to prepare himself as best he could. And when the celebra-tion was over, he would always spend fifteen minutes on his knees, absorbed in thanksgiving.

◆ ◆ ◆

Another striking thing was the attention with which he would say the words of the Mass and the seriousness with which he would perform the eucharistic gestures. He was obviously trying to help people grasp clearly the message the words conveyed and the symbolic meaning the actions were supposed to express. He wanted the faithful attending the Eucharist to feel that they were experiencing a truly sacred moment.

He always made a point of not celebrating alone. Whether he was saying Mass in his private chapel or somewhere else, such as in a parish or in the cathedral, he always invited other people to celebrate with him, so that the Mass would always be a community event. In other words, he was trying to be faithful to the principle that the priest doesn't celebrate the Eucharist alone, but with the people of God, who also take part in it—through Christ and with Christ.

Wojtyla's style of celebrating was already enough to make it clear why he followed the inspiration of the Curé of Ars, Jean-Marie Vianney, in shedding the attitude of the old-fashioned clericalist priest. It explained, in other words, why he didn't consider priesthood as membership in some class or caste, but as a way of being present among the people of God, in direct contact with his fellow Christians. The point, then, was that for him the priest was first and foremost a steward of the mysteries of God. And so the Mass came to be the center of his life and of his day.

His private chapel was his special meeting place with God. He tried to spend as much time in the chapel as possible. If he was at home, he would stay there until eleven in the morning. The chapel was where he would carry on a dialogue with God and listen to what the Lord had to say to him. Sometimes the sisters who looked after the residence would peek into the chapel out of curiosity, and they always found him in the same position: prostrate on the floor, immersed in prayer. He also used to work in the chapel when he had to draft documents, such as the texts of the Kraków Synod or his pastoral letters. He had an interesting way of marking the pages. Instead of using page numbers, he would write prayer verses. So you see, work was also a form of intense prayer for him.

Along with prayer, he placed a lot of emphasis on Confession. The most important thing about the sacrament for him wasn't the revelation of your sins, but God's forgiveness and remission of them. The main thing for him, in other words, was the grace Confession gives you, the strength it offers you to lead an upright and virtuous life. He himself would go to Confession once a week. He would also confess before major feast days and special liturgical seasons. Even after becoming a bishop, he would go to the Franciscan church for Confession and get in line with the other penitents.

Besides, when he was an assistant pastor at Saint Florian's years earlier, Father Karol had relied on prayer and Confession as the foundation of his—at that time—truly pioneering pastoral work with college students. Of course, he also cultivated close relations with the professors, being convinced that the future of Poland—this was the mid-1950s and Communist domination was now in full swing—would depend on the education and formation of academics. And that meant that a lot depended on faculty members doing their part.

✦ ✦ ✦

That's right. When he was at Saint Florian's, Father Karol gathered together a group of college students and became their
leader and spiritual guide. The first thing he taught the kids was
the right way to pray. He urged them to participate in the sacraments, especially Mass. He gave them lessons in theological and
philosophical anthropology, but also in how to live in community
and how to respect others. He would take them on trips. They
would go hiking in the mountains or camping. This came to be
known as the "hiker's apostolate," and in order to avoid the
watchful eye of the police, Wojtyla would dress in civil garb and
the kids would call him *"wujek"* (uncle). So he managed to form
a group of people united, of course, around the Word of God, but
also around ideas, around a shared concern for their country, and
around a desire to help one another grow up.

*Wojtyla remained faithful to his commitment to young people
even after becoming a bishop and a cardinal. During the year, he
would meet with them for days of retreat, reflection, and prayer.
He would join them on pilgrimages to the major shrines, such as
Kalwaria Zebrzydowska and Czestochowa, where, as he put it,
he would go to hear the Mother's "heartbeat." In fact, he accompanied them throughout the many stages of their lives:
blessing their marriages, baptizing their children, spending time
with their families, while always caring for them as a real pastor.
He was a friend, of course, but he was first a father, a spiritual
guide and pastor.*

Well, this "milieu," or community of laypeople (the Polish name
for it is Srodowisko, which doesn't mean quite the same thing),

was made up of people who remained faithful to the path Wojtyla had shown them and the direction they'd received from him. And these people then went on to exercise important functions in society and culture, as university professors, doctors, engineers, et cetera. And today we're seeing a third generation of mature, committed Catholic citizens, living out the same spirit of love of God and neighbor as their grandparents who were part of the Srodowisko group.

The Srodowisko group also included holy people like Jerzy Ciesielski. Jerzy was an engineer. He had been teaching at Kraków Polytech, but he accepted a job in Africa, at the University of Khartoum. While he was sailing down the Nile, there was a terrible accident, and almost everyone on board his ship was killed, including Jerzy and two of his children. Only one of his daughters and a friend of hers escaped. It was a great loss. He was a young man, and he was upright, hardworking, and deeply religious. His life was, and still is, an example to others. In fact, the cause for his beatification has already made it to the Congregation for the Causes of Saints.

Jerzy was one of Wojtyla's favorite friends. When Jerzy died, the archbishop wrote that faith had been "the normal measure of his duties."

It was laypeople like Ciesielski whom, as archbishop, Wojtyla would involve in the major undertakings of the diocese. He was a big delegator and he gave the people he appointed for a certain mission or charge a lot of room to exercise responsibility. Of course, he would be the one to coordinate everything personally, to provide the guidelines, and to put new energy into the work of evangelization. This personal involvement enabled him to stay in immediate contact with people. His pastoral visits to the

*parishes—especially those, in fact—did so, as well. For him,
these visits weren't just canonical visitations or official inspec-
tions prescribed by the administrative handbook; they were his
way of entering into the life of a given parish community as its
bishop and pastor.*

That's why he always tried to stay as long as possible. So much
so, in fact, that his visits would sometimes last for weeks. He
would participate in the liturgical celebrations and in all of the
parish priests' tasks. He visited the sick in their homes—in fact,
he was the one who took the initiative to set up a ministry for
sick people in the diocese. He would visit the families, of which
there were many, including the priests' families. When he said
Mass, he would invite couples to renew their marriage vows. Actually, he wanted to stay separately with each family in order to
see them up close and to pray with them. And then there were
the young people. He couldn't visit them at school because the
authorities wouldn't allow it. And so it was in the church that he
would see the children receiving religious instruction and would
talk with their teachers—or at least the ones who were brave
enough to show up. Not everyone was. Not everyone could risk
losing the job they held.

*At the time, Poland was still a land in chains. And God was a
name that couldn't be spoken in public—a forbidden name.*

3.

Turning Point:
Vatican II

When the council began on October 11, 1962, Karol Wojtyla had one of the last seats in the assembly. Just a few months before the opening of the council, he had been chosen as the capitulary vicar and temporary administrator of the Kraków diocese. But he was still only an auxiliary bishop. Which is precisely why he was consigned to the back, near the entrance to Saint Peter's Basilica. But even from the back, he could see and hear what was going on. And during the first session, he preferred to listen. And to learn.

As soon as he heard the news that there was going to be a council, young Bishop Wojtyla was very open about his enthusiasm for John XXIII's plans. He wasn't afraid of new things.

Wojtyla had become convinced that the Church needed a different approach, especially for dealing with issues like ecumenism, liturgical renewal, and more active lay involvement in the life of the Church. This last topic was one which a person like him—

who partly owed his own growth in religious faith to two laypeo-
ple, his father and a catechist friend—naturally considered es-
pecially important. In fact, he believed that the priest's role was
to serve the laity and that both the laity and the clergy were es-
sential components of Christ's Church.

From the day it started on October 11, 1962, attending the
council was like going to a big school for in-depth study of doctrine and pastoral aggiornamento. And Bishop Wojtyla decided
that the whole diocese would get involved spiritually in the
council's work. He kept in touch with priests and seminarians.
He tried to generate interest among intellectuals. He made sure
that everyone was informed about the topics debated on the assembly floor and about what was in the conciliar documents. So
those of us in Kraków were very much involved in what was happening in Rome.

Meanwhile, for Wojtyla himself, the council was an opportunity for constant sharing of insights about pastoral or social issues, for getting acquainted with new trends in theology, and for
meeting great scholars and experts, such as the famous Jesuit
Henri de Lubac (who had extemely positive things to say about
the cultivation and intelligence of the auxiliary bishop of Kraków). Wojtyla also met well-known German-speaking theologians such as Fathers Joseph Ratzinger and Hans Küng, as well as
their French-speaking counterparts, such as Yves Congar, Jean
Daniélou, Marie-Dominique Chenu, and Antoine Wenger. And
then there were contacts with outstanding bishops like John Krol
from the United States, Gabriel-Marie Garonne from France,
and Joachim Meisner, Joseph Höffner, and Alfred Bengsch from
Germany.

Above all, though, I should recall Wojtyla's friendship with

Cardinal Franz König, the archbishop of Vienna, who deserves a lot of praise for what he did to open up Poland's borders. He was one of the first cardinals to defy the Communist regime and go to Poland in order to make contact with people inside the country. And that was very important, because during the Stalinist era, every contact with the Apostolic See was considered to be an act of espionage. And the people in contact with Rome were condemned as spies, as if they were enemies of the Polish state and the Communist system.

The Berlin Wall began to go up on the night of August 13, 1961. Its purpose was to prevent the continual exodus of those living in East Germany. This marked the beginning of a new phase of the Cold War. Moscow reined in its satellites, and the campaign for atheism flared up again even in Catholic Poland. Consequently, many bishops could not get a passport to go to Rome and participate in the council. The only ones who were allowed to go were the primate, Cardinal Stefan Wyszynski, and the young auxiliary bishop of Kraków, who, along with a few others, would take part in all four sessions.

Even so, the Polish episcopate still managed to play a big role in raising awareness about the situation of the Church under communism. The Polish bishops helped people realize that, in spite of the persecution, in spite of the aggressive atheism, the Church under communism was still alive and dynamic, with full seminaries, new forms of pastoral ministry, and an increasingly huge involvement of the laity in Church life. In Poland, the Church was a support for oppressed people deprived of the chance to speak. And, when you consider how the rights of the person were curtailed, the Church was the only zone of freedom. It was only within the Church community that people could feel genuinely free. The Church was the only forum where an independent culture, a Christian culture, had a chance to develop.

By the time the third session of Vatican II opened, Wojtyla, who in the meantime had been named archbishop, had also received a noticeable elevation in status: He was now seated much closer to the altar. And this gain in personal visibility coincided with another change: He emerged from his initial phase of listening and entered into a new phase of creativity and active participation. He thus began to speak more frequently on the council floor, talking, for example, about the Pastoral Constitution, Gaudium et Spes, one of the council's major innovations. Never before had the Church shown such a clear and intense interest in the problems of contemporary man, or in the issues facing humanity in its historical development. After Gaudium et Spes, the Church would no longer go out to meet the world with the expectation of finding only an enemy to be combated.

In this respect especially, Archbishop Wojtyla was the prophet of a new era for the Church, both in Poland and in the world at large. In fact, he was the kind of bishop who not only wasn't afraid of the world but went out to meet it in the strength of the Gospel message, without prematurely ruling out anything. And he could do that precisely because he was able to recognize the great values of the contemporary world. And so he thought that if those values were given the right direction, if they were sanctified, they could be received and welcomed by the Church. Actually, he thought that they needed to become a resource for the Church.

♦ ♦ ♦

Then there was the huge question of religious freedom. Thanks to his background, which obliged him to deal day in and day out with an authoritarian and oppressive regime, Wojtyla was able to make a decisively important contribution to the discussion. On one hand, he helped the council get beyond a concept of negative freedom conceived as nothing but mere tolerance. On the other hand, he argued that if religious freedom is the highest expression of the dignity of the person, it is a right that cannot be ignored, much less denied, by public authorities or states.

Archbishop Wojtyla brought a twofold innovation onto the council floor. In essence, it was this: reassertion of the centrality of the person within a robust Christocentric framework; and engaging the world with the Gospel message, coupled with a defense of the rights of man, especially the right to freedom of conscience and religion.

Years down the road, his pontificate would synthesize those two things: what he experienced in Poland and the fruit of his experience at Vatican II. This is yet another proof that having to live under communism didn't weaken his approach to the Church, to ecumenism, and to social issues, but, rather, strengthened it. It thus prepared him for his universal mission, prepared him to be an authoritative dialogue partner both for other churches and for today's world.

On one hand, then, Wojtyla was able to create an awareness of, and confidence in, the churches of Eastern Europe, which had defied their circumstances and remained spiritually free and faithful to the Gospel. On the other hand, he showed how the

Polish Church especially was equipped to deal not only with the problems created by Communist oppression but also with the problems, especially the moral problems, that would later arrive from the so-called liberal world of the West.

For Karol Wojtyla, then, Vatican II was a real turning point. He used to say that he was "indebted to the council." And it is true that he returned from Rome with an enormous number of new experiences and ideas. He even wrote a book about them: Sources of Renewal. *And he used these experiences and ideas as a basis for rethinking his own ministry as a bishop and then for reshaping the life of the Church in Kraków by means of a diocesan synod.*

The fact that he did that shows that Archbishop Wojtyla wasn't afraid of the council. Just the opposite, in fact. He eagerly looked forward to the developments it might foster in the Catholic community. That eagerness is also what prompted him to translate the fruits of Vatican II into a pastoral plan adapted to the Polish situation. He proceeded in this undertaking with great prudence, of course, but also without prejudices. Above all, he proceeded with great hopes and great joy. The period of implementing the decisions of the council was a happy time not only for the archbishop of Kraków but for the whole archdiocese and the Church in Poland.

4.

The Millennium Crisis

In Gaudium et Spes, the Church openly acknowledged for the first time the sins committed by Christians down through the centuries against the truth of God and the truth about man. This acknowledgment kicked off the process of rethinking and repentance that would later come to be called the "purification of memory." It also gave the Polish bishops an idea.

And so a proposal was born in the Polish episcopate. It was first put on the table by Archbishop Boleslaw Kominek, but it immediately won the approval of the primate and the backing of other bishops, especially Wojtyla. In fact, he would be one of those responsible for implementing it.

We are talking, of course, about the proposal to send a letter to the German bishops to promote reconciliation between the two nations and their citizens. "We extend our hands to you, forgiving you and asking you to forgive us," the letter read. Nor did the bishops gloss over any of the past, whether it was Hitler's concentration camps and the Nazi crematoria, or the controversy about Poland's western border and the sufferings of thou-

sands of German refugees turned out of their homes immedi-
ately following the war.

That act of asking for and extending forgiveness was an extremely profound human and Christian gesture. And it was also
a farsighted one, at least in terms of the German episcopate's response, because just a few years later, Poland and West Germany
would come to an agreement about the Oder-Neisse border. So
things came together in an extremely important way and the result was a kind of Magna Carta in the history of the two countries, not just from the point of view of the Church but, first of
all, from the point of view of national politics.

It was in those very same months, though, that a reactionary
chill began to descend on the Soviet Empire. Khrushchev was
tossed out of office and the new bosses in the Kremlin, especially
Brezhnev, enforced an incredibly hard line. At the same time the
Soviets were making multiple gestures of détente in order to con-
vince the outside world of their wish for "peaceful coexistence,"
they were repressing every form of opposition at home in an at-
tempt to stifle the winds of change. Obviously, Moscow couldn't
allow any discussion of an issue like that concerning the
German-Polish border, which it claimed sole authority to decide.
  So when the orders came down, the Polish regime dutifully
launched an assault on the episcopate, accusing it of "interfer-
ence in foreign affairs" and of having "absolved" the Nazis of
their crimes. The press, too, joined in with a relentless campaign
of its own, which initially succeeded in convincing a lot of
Catholics and even a lot of anti-Communists.

◆   ◆   ◆

The charge that carried the most weight with people was that the bishops were unpatriotic. The accusation was completely false, but the authorities had an easy time milking the anti-German sentiment that was still deeply rooted among Poles of many different classes. This is why Archbishop Wojtyla felt he had to speak up. So in his homily for that year's Corpus Christi celebrations in Kraków, he issued his now-famous defense of the Polish episcopate: "If anyone is going to call our consciences to account, it's not them; if anyone is going to teach us patriotism, it's not them."

The attacks weren't over, though. There was an explosion of anti-clericalism in the diet. There were fascistlike action squads and demonstrations with huge signs denouncing the bishops as enemies of the state. Sometimes the protesters stood right under the windows of Cardinal Wyszynski and Archbishop Wojtyla.

The workers of the Solvay chemical plant, where Karol Wojtyla had worked as a young man during the Nazi occupation, viciously attacked the archbishop of Kraków, obviously at the behest of someone in the regime. The newspapers published a slanderous letter, signed "the workers of the chemical industry," which the archbishop himself had never received. Wojtyla answered with firm resolution. He responded to his accusers by insisting that he was a "man who has been wronged, wronged by exposure to public accusation and slander put forward by men who have not bothered to examine honestly either the facts or my real motives."

But all of the major newspapers refused to publish his response. A small local daily was the only periodical that picked it up.

◆ ◆ ◆

That was a very difficult time. But the primate managed to make a very astute statement just when it was needed most. He organized a ceremony at the Jasna Góra monastery, and the memory of that event became an unforgettable one for all Poles. Standing before a huge crowd, Cardinal Wyszynski had someone read out the most controversial passage from the letter to the German bishops. Then, after the recitation of the Our Father, he said in a loud voice, "We, the bishops of Poland, together with the people of God, say, We forgive!" The whole crowd answered with a single huge shout that felt like the rumbling of thunder: "We forgive!"

Meanwhile, a new year had started. It was 1966. And it just so happened that 1966 was also the one thousandth anniversary of the Baptism of Poland and the foundation of the Polish state. The millennium festivities scheduled for 1966 would cap off a nine-year-long novena that Cardinal Wyszynski had initiated in 1957 to prepare for the event. But what had been planned as an occasion for a huge religious and patriotic celebration led instead to a dramatic rupture between the Church and the Communist regime. Already furious on account of the letter to the German bishops, the Warsaw government decided to boycott the religious celebrations of the millennium and to promote exclusively secular ones instead.

The showdown began when Cardinal Wyszynski's passport was withdrawn. Then Pope Paul VI was refused permission to visit the country and the borders were closed right at the high point of the ceremonies. And since the image of the Black Madonna (a copy of the original one blessed by Pius XII) was being carried through the streets of every city and village in Poland, the police had a lot of opportunity to make constant trouble.

They would arbitrarily require a change of itinerary in order to make it harder for the faithful to participate. Or else they would order that the image be returned to Czestochowa, so that the pilgrims had to continue the procession with just a candle burning inside the now-empty picture frame.

The celebrations began on April 14 in Gniezno. They marked the day, one thousand years earlier, when Mieszko I was baptized. Well, on the same day the authorities organized a counterdemonstration. The secretary of the Communist party, Gomulka, made a speech in the main square of Gniezno at exactly the same time the primate was addressing the faithful assembled around the cathedral. The people were forced to take part in the state-organized demonstration, but as soon as it was over, they ran to hear Cardinal Wyszynski. They had an inkling that it was a sensitive moment and so they wanted to show that they were with the Church, which was the only force working to promote freedom at the time.

Let me be clear: This wasn't an opposition movement struggling against the Communist regime. In fact, the Church avoided confrontation with the state authorities. It simply tried to carry out its specific mission, taking advantage of the opportunities it had for pastoral work. And in this case, it was merely trying to defend and safeguard this same mission.

So in spite of the obstacles and the official refusals, in spite of the counterpropaganda, the religious celebrations sparked enormous enthusiasm everywhere, along with a very significant revival of Christian practice and a massive return to the sacraments. The same thing happened in Kraków. On the evening of May 7, the day before a big celebration of the millennium, the authorities organized an alternative secular event. They were betting on the undeniable appeal of another anniversary: the twenty-first anniversary of the end of World War II in Europe. A lot of people, then, were convinced that there would be only a small turnout for the Mass the next day. What happened instead?

All night long, thousands upon thousands of people thronged the Wawel Cathedral, where the image of the Madonna was displayed. An unforgettable experience! And the archbishop made a vigorous defense of religious freedom, protesting against all the restrictions—in this case, the issue was interference in liturgical matters—the regime placed on the life of the Church. He spoke very courageously, but also very logically. In other words, he didn't provoke. He based his criticism on definite, specific arguments that demonstrated the illegality of the acts committed by the Communist authorities. He defended the human person and fought for both the Church's and the individual's right to freedom.

On August 26, the closing Mass of the millennium was celebrated in Czestochowa. The Pope wasn't there, since he had been denied permission to visit Poland. But his portrait was, surrounded by a wreath of red and white roses. And there was an impressively large crowd in attendance—more than a million people. That day, there was no doubt as to who had emerged the victor in what had been an extraordinarily tough conflict between the Church and the Communist party.

5.

Wyszynski and Wojtyla

In all the millennium celebrations, Wojtyla was always next to Wyszynski, always at his side, always attentive, always solicitous. Yet he never took the spotlight, but consistently let Wyszynski do the talking. This was an eloquent sign both of the archbishop of Kraków's deep respect for the primate and of the absence of any disagreement, much less division, between them.

The authorities, though, did try to sow discord between them and turn them against each other. And that's exactly why, as archbishop, Wojtyla not only always remained absolutely faithful to the primate but also took special pains to demonstrate in a clear, obvious, and conspicuous way that they were united and followed the same line of action. In fact, he would visit the primate during holidays, spend a lot time with him, and support him publicly at difficult moments.

The only people who hadn't caught on were the Communist bosses. Or maybe they were so convinced the opposite was the case that they couldn't bring themselves to admit the truth. In other words, they clung to their long-cherished hope that one day they might see Wyszynski replaced by Wojtyla. They regarded the primate as a more formidable foe on account of his tough anti-Communist stand, while they thought the archbishop was an enlightened progressive, or at least deemed him to be more malleable and open to dialogue than Wyszynski.

Witness the fact that when Wojtyla was made archbishop of Kraków, the number-two man in the Communist party, Zenon Kliszko, publicly boasted that Wyszynski had submitted two lists of candidates without Wojtyla's name—and that he, Kliszko, had rejected both of them, thus ensuring Wojtyla's nomination. The truth is that the primate had probably omitted Wojtyla's name on purpose, so as to avoid automatically ruining the prospects of the candidate that he actually thought was the right one for the see of Kraków.

And yet the idea of creating opposition between the two highest representatives of the Church cropped up again after the millennium celebrations, when Wojtyla was created cardinal in 1967.

Speaking of the nomination as cardinal . . . The archbishop was on a pastoral visit in Brzezie when the newspapers and the radio announced the news. When he got back to Kraków on Monday, he said, "Well, that's news to me!" Then he started looking through the correspondence he'd received from the Apostolic See. It was then he realized that the letter notifying him of his nomination had been lying in the stack of letters for at least three days.

Well, when Archbishop Wojtyla was created cardinal, L'Unità, the newspaper of the Italian Communist party, published a re-

port from Warsaw stating that his nomination to the cardinalate could "be the first step toward eroding, or at least curtailing, the total monopoly over the Polish Church hitherto exercised by Cardinal Wyszynski."

The secret police said the same thing in a confidential report outlining a strategic plan to provoke division between the two cardinals: "We need to continue using every opportunity to show our hostility toward Wyszynski, but without forcing Wojtyla to show solidarity with Wyszynski."

Of course, the attempt to destroy the unity of the Church in every way and at every level was a familiar tactic with the Communist regime. They had already tried to dismember the Church at the diocesan level by driving a wedge between the priests and the bishop. But it hadn't worked. Only a few priests had, for different reasons, caved in and become so-called patriotic priests. But those were really just a few isolated cases. And now the regime was at it again, only this time the aim was to create disunity among the leaders of the Church.

But the attempt was doomed to failure, because it was based on a completely false assessment of the situation. There had never been even a single episode of discord or a single reason for dissension. In addition, the two cardinals had found a way of dividing up their roles and tasks that made it extremely easy for them to work together as pastors. The primate set the direction, the overall strategy, while Wojtyla articulated the theory behind it. Wyszynski devoted himself completely to the Church and the Polish social and political situation; Wojtyla, partly because he was younger and better at foreign languages, visited the Polish communities abroad.

The most obvious proof of their excellent relations was the fact that the archbishop of Kraków never failed to demonstrate his great respect for, and transparent loyalty to, the primate. For example, when Wyszynski was once again denied a visa to go to Rome for the Synod of Bishops, Cardinal Wojtyla showed his solidarity by forgoing the trip, as well. That was the coup de grâce that ended the Communist leaders' plan to drive a wedge between the two cardinals.

As soon as the first plan failed, though, they thought up another one. The new plan was the complete opposite of the first one. This time, they tried a tactic they called "role reversal." From that point on, they began to speak of Wyszynski as a patriot who understood the Polish situation, whereas they called Wojtyla an internationalist who was clueless about Poland and accused him of being unpatriotic—indeed, an enemy of the Polish Communist system, someone who opposed the good of the state. In other words, they directed all their hatred against him.

Needless to say, Cardinal Wojtyla didn't react. He never sought confrontation, much less conflict. Instead, he sought an objective dialogue based on the same arguments as always: the freedom of the Church to proclaim the Gospel and engage in its apostolate, together with the freedom of man, both individually and socially, spiritually and materially. But the point, of course, is that the freedom of man is exactly what the Communist authorities hated most. And by the same logic, they hated the people who defended it.

In Poland, the protests continued to come and go in cycles. In Poznań in 1956, it was the workers; in 1968, it was the students and the intellectuals; then, on the Baltic coast in 1970, it was the workers again. Cardinal Wyszynski called these protests "the little revolutions." "Revolutions" because they laid bare the fact that Marxist ideology, and even Polish-style "real socialism," was crumbling. But the revolutions were "little" because they always failed to change the social and economic situation—except among the Communist party brass. In fact, things always got worse; the only noticeable change was a tightening of the repression.

As a result, an increasingly large number of people were stripped of their freedom. These same people now turned to Wojtyla as their last refuge, as their sole protector and defender.

By this point, the archbishop of Kraków had become a reference point for a lot of different groups in society. He supported the demands of the workers. He protected the young, the intellectuals, the teachers who were forbidden to go to church, the scholars who were constantly being censored. Not to mention the dissidents, the persecuted. And, as always, he wasn't acting politically, but in the name of the Gospel, in the name of the dignity of the human person.

Another persecuted group consisted of the few Jews who were still left in Poland following World War II. After the student unrest in 1968, they were accused of hatching the "plot." This was a vile accusation, because in truth they had nothing to do with it. It was just a pretext to divert attention from the attack on the revisionists and to inflame nationalist sentiment among the people. But the Communist bosses, starting with Gomulka, whose wife was Jewish no less, lost control of the situation. What they got was an all-out anti-Semitic campaign. Between the Jews who were forced into exile and the ones who left the country volun-

tarily, Poland lost its entire Jewish elite, which numbered about fifteen thousand people.

Cardinal Wojtyla, who was a champion of interreligious dialogue, had enjoyed good relations with the Jewish community for some time. When he was on pastoral visits in the parishes, he often stopped at the Jewish cemeteries. But when he went to visit the synagogue in Kraków's Kazimierz neighborhood at the end of February 1969, he wanted his gesture to be as conspicuous as possible, precisely to express his and the Catholic Church's solidarity with all Jews because of the renewed persecution they were being forced to suffer.

Something amazing had happened four years earlier in Rome. Wojtyla had run into Jerzy Kluger, one of his dearest Jewish friends from Wadowice. They hadn't seen each other since 1938, when they had gotten together with their other classmates to celebrate high school graduation. But then the war broke out.

Each had thought the other was dead, but then they unexpectedly found each other again.

6.

The Cross of Nowa Huta

It took almost twenty years to build the church at Nowa Huta. The period of construction coincided exactly with Karol Wojtyla's tenure as archbishop of Kraków, stretching from his consecration to the eve of his election to the papacy. The two stories continually interweave, moreover, and each one sheds light on the other. The tale of Nowa Huta reflects how Wojtyla lived out his role as bishop—that is, as the shepherd of a local church and the guide and defender of his people—and, at the same time, how he dealt with a power based exclusively on oppression and atheistic ideology.

The Nowa Huta experience permanently shaped Wojtyla's pastoral program as an archbishop, just as it permanently shaped the personality of the future Pope as an unyielding defender of human rights, of the rights of freedom of conscience and religion. In fact, you could say that the battle Wojtyla would wage as Pope on behalf of man, of the dignity of the human person, began right there at Nowa Huta, his first test as a young, newly consecrated bishop.

Kraków already had 700,000 inhabitants by the end of the 1950s, and it had gone on expanding at the edges into an ever more complex spiderweb of new suburbs. New neighborhoods were springing up like mushrooms, but most of them had no place of worship, since the Communist authorities refused to grant the necessary building permits.

Nowa Huta was a huge steel town. It was socialism's answer to Catholic Kraków. The planners wanted Nowa Huta to be a city without God, and when they built it, they intentionally left no room for a church. But the people who came from the surrounding villages—especially from Tarnów—were deeply religious and wanted to have God in their midst. They wanted the chance to live near a church, to have a normal religious life and normal pastoral care.

So the request for permission to build a church wasn't a way of picking a fight. The faithful simply wanted the right to build a house of God for celebrating Mass.

Bienczyce, a residential neighborhood of Nowa Huta, already had a chapel. After the authorities had repeatedly denied them permission to build a church, the inhabitants went to the chapel site and erected an extremely tall cross pointing toward the sky. But the regime interpreted the cross as a provocation, a challenge, as if it were the first step toward abolishing the Communist system. So the cross was pulled down. This immediately triggered a reaction among Catholics. There were violent clashes with the police, which resulted in injuries and many arrests.

In retrospect, we can say that it was the first time believers clashed with a Communist regime in a socialist city. Nowa Huta was a capital of the working class—and it answered the authority of the state with a resounding no. The people said, "We have rights!" They demanded the right to freedom of conscience, the right to freedom of religion. Nowa Huta was the beginning of a new strategy based on resistance. The resistance had a religious impetus, but for the first time it was being actively applied against the decisions of the authorities. Nowa Huta was the first act in a long struggle to defend the freedom and dignity of the people, the people of God.

And it was also the first big test for Bishop Wojtyla. Since Archbishop Baziak was seriously ill, Wojtyla, though still a young auxiliary bishop when the affair started, had to manage the whole business by himself. On the one hand, he had to try to settle the serious problem just mentioned. On the other hand, though, he had to be very careful not to create another one by provoking an escalation of the hostilities.

At that point, at least, the enterprise seemed desperate. And yet Wojtyla pulled it off. Keeping a steady focus on principles and rights, he started up negotiations with both central and provincial authorities. But he never yielded an inch. And he never failed to support the Christian community's legitimate demands.

As a result, the government was obliged to give in. They finally granted permission to build the church, though not on the same spot where the cross had been erected, but in another part of Nowa Huta.

Moreover, Wojtyla continued to visit the steel yards, as he had already done at Bienczyce. He even showed up on Christmas Eve to celebrate an open-air Mass, despite heavy snowfall and subzero temperatures.

◆　◆　◆

That's the story behind the building of the Ark of the Lord, the magnificent new church symbolizing Poland's freedom from the myth of cities without God. The people understood that their sense of national identity didn't depend on the coercive power of a regime incapable of representing Polish society, but on the men and women of Poland itself. The church was dedicated on May 15, 1977, after twenty years of waiting, anxious uncertainty, and struggle. And it was dedicated in the presence of the bishop—by now a cardinal—who had bequeathed his name forever to Nowa Huta.

And Nowa Huta wasn't the only workers' city that became a front in the battle to build new churches. Another one was Mistrzejowice, whose heroic parish priest, Josef Kurzeja, was mercilessly harassed by the Communist officials and died of a heart attack at age thirty-nine. There was also Ciesiec, where the parishioners themselves decided to build a church, despite the wishes of the political commissar. And Wojtyla sent his secretary, Father Stanislaw, to show his solidarity and his support of the people's right to their own house of worship.

They started building the church on a Saturday. Everyone—men, women, and children—worked throughout the entire day, and by evening the church was finished. Of course it was a very simple church—but so much effort, so much toil went into putting it up! The local authorities shut off the power and blocked the road into town. In spite of that, the people stayed where they were. At night, they lighted the building site by burning rubber tires. They had arranged to take turns putting on the finishing touches, and standing guard.

◆ ◆ ◆

Such was daily life in Poland under the Communist regime. People had to fight to build places of worship. They also had to fight for the formation of the clergy, since the government had shut down the theology department at Kraków's Jagellionian University, which was subsequently turned into a secular institution completely dependent on the state.

The goal was to control the education of future priests by making them subservient to Marxist ideology, which would then ensure their obedience and submissiveness to the system. This meant that the final target was the annihilation of the Catholic religion. This is why Cardinal Wojtyla worked hard to obtain pontifical status for the new theological school, which had subsequently been established within the Kraków seminary. With pontifical status, the Kraków school could grant academic degrees, thereby creating a cultivated, well-qualified clergy that didn't have any problems dealing with laypeople.

A free, independent, highly cultured Church would be equipped to face the challenges posed by ideologies of whatever stripe. It would thus be in a position to retrieve the patrimony of Christian culture that had enabled Poland to maintain its own identity and to survive—even when it was erased from the map of Europe.

In those years, they began the Tygodnie Kultury Chrześcijańskiej (Christian Culture Weeks), and the cardinal was the financial patron. In the same way, he tried (anonymously, of course) to help university professors, scholars, and prominent figures in the arts and the theater who had lost their jobs because they wouldn't bow to Communist ideology.

As a matter of principle, the archbishop never collected his salary from the Curia, which was just a token amount anyway. The offerings he received from parish priests and the royalties from his publications went entirely to support his various undertakings and for charity. He lived in poverty, and he never needed anything. He had only one black outer garment. It was pretty flimsy, so he would wear an insulated liner underneath it in the winter.

Such was the state of things under Marxism. There was a daily struggle for the survival of religion and the Church and for that of the Polish people and their country.

7.

"How Could I Fail to Speak Out?"

Cardinal Wojtyla traveled a lot in those years.

He began to visit the Polish communities in the diaspora. His journeys took him to places like Chicago, where he met with an association of former Polish prisoners of Auschwitz. He had brought them a gift: a handful of dirt from the death camp.

He also made pilgrimages. He went to the Holy Land and recounted the trip to his priests in a beautiful letter that read like a kind of spiritual reporter's notebook. He told them about his deep emotion at seeing the "point," the exact place God chose to enter the world at a precise moment of human history.

In addition, the archbishop was frequently invited to take part in conferences or conventions, or to speak at major events, like the eucharistic congresses in Melbourne—where he met Mother Teresa for the first time—and Philadelphia.

Those trips were an opportunity for him to get to know what life was like on other continents. They expanded his horizons beyond Europe and familiarized him with America, Asia, Oceania, and Africa. Above all, they were a chance for him to understand the people who lived in other climes and in widely varying situations. What is more, I think those trips played an important role in preparing him for the tasks he would subsequently carry out as shepherd of the universal Church.

And it goes without saying that Wojtyla had frequent appointments at the Vatican. He was part of the commission on the birth-control issue. He was a member of many different Roman congregations. And when he returned from Rome, he would always note with satisfaction how international the Roman Curia was becoming in the wake of Vatican II. And how much less "Latin" or "Eurocentric" the process of writing documents was than it had been in the past.

Every time Wojtyla went to Rome, Paul VI would grant him an audience. The Pope admired the young archbishop of Kraków for his deep spirituality, his apostolic courage, his learning and cultivation, and his serenity of mind, as well as for his unfailing faithfulness and loyalty. Paul VI showed his goodwill toward Wojtyla on a number of occasions. Finally, he invited Wojtyla to preach the 1976 Lenten meditations in the Vatican. That was a great honor, but also a heavy responsibility.

Wojtyla's meditations were inspired by the words of Simeon: "Behold, he is set for the fall and the rising again of many in Israel and as a sign of contradiction." Applying this to the present day, Wojtyla noted that the Church itself, the Pope, and the bishops, as well as priests, members of religious orders, and believers in general were going to share Christ's fate. They were destined to become "signs of contradiction" in a world that was trying, either by force or by silence, to deny the truth of God and about God.

He spoke of the dangers posed both by the increasingly secularized and consumeristic society of the West and by the entrenched atheistic system of the East. He then went on to describe the tactic deployed by the Communist states in their war on religion: "[Do] everything possible to avoid creating new martyrs. Persecution, then, is the order of the day, but, for the sake of appearances, there is no persecution, but full religious freedom."

That wasn't just rhetoric. It arose from the daily experience that Wojtyla unfortunately had to deal with as archbishop of Kraków. The sad fact is that the state's campaign of silent persecution against groups, associations, and individuals went on creating new victims on a daily basis.

For example, one boy, a student at a certain vocational school, wore a cross around his neck, as a lot of people did at the time. The school authorities told him, "You'd better take off that cross. Otherwise, you're banned from campus, and what's more, you can't take part in any of the training programs." The boy refused and was expelled. His mother was called in. But she held her ground, insisting, "I'm proud of my son."

Another episode involved a lady who lent the parish a room in her apartment to use for catechism class. When the authorities found out, they called her in and threatened to take away her job.

Then there was the engineer who was on his way to becoming the director of an important factory. He had an outstanding résumé and was obviously the ideal candidate for such a responsible job. But he was told he would have to go to a certain room for an interview. He went in, told them he was a believer, and the interview ended there. He didn't get the position.

Although for obvious reasons he didn't reveal the names of the victims, Cardinal Wojtyla spoke out against all of this repression in his speeches and homilies. He openly protested against those who were trying to erase God from the depth of man's soul.

He spoke out in 1976, for example, when yet again the authorities heavily restricted the parade route for the Corpus Christi procession.

"I'm often chided," he said, "for talking about these things. But how could I fail to speak out? How could I fail to write about them? How could I stand by and do nothing? I am a bishop, and so I must be the first servant of this cause, of this great cause that is man himself."

It was inevitable, then, that he would become the "bogeyman" of the regime. And they did everything they could to impede him, not only trying to block his pastoral work but also to intimidate him psychologically. They spied on him and kept him under constant surveillance. They wanted to make him feel that they were constantly on his back, bearing down on him with the full weight of their power, their "omnipotence."

The entire archbishop's residence, including the study, the dining room, the parlor, and even the cardinal's bedroom, was bugged; the whole place was "wallpapered" with listening devices. They were in the telephones, of course, but they were also stuck behind the wall coverings, or under the furniture.

We knew perfectly well that electronic ears were eavesdropping on us. Plus, the spies were so incompetent that we couldn't help knowing. A party of workers would just show up without warning and tell us that the telephone was out of order or that there was a problem with the electrical system. That was their ruse for planting the bugs.

The cardinal even made a joke out of it. He would speak in a loud voice to make sure they could really hear, and he would tell them what he wanted them to think. But when he had sensitive conversations, he would leave the residence. For example, if the secretary of the Bishops' Conference, Bronislaw Dabrowski, would visit, they would go talk in a nearby wood. If foreign bishops came to visit, he would even take them to the mountains.

Wojtyla was systematically watched; every one of his sermons was recorded and then dissected line by line. And whenever he left the residence, even for a long trip, he was tailed by the secret police. They were always there, always on duty, watching from the other side of Franciszkańska Street. And as soon as the archbishop's car left the building, the agents would glide along behind in their sinister black vehicles. In fact, he used to wave at them or even bless them as he was about to leave. He used to call them "my guardian angels."

Wojtyla's driver, a wonderful man called Mucha, was great at throwing them off the trail. Once when the archbishop had a meeting he wanted to keep secret, Mucha came up with a maneuver worthy of 007. He suddenly stepped on the gas and swerved into a line of cars, giving the cardinal time to jump out and get into another vehicle. Then Mucha continued on his way, with the spies in tow behind him.

This went on even after the Kraków years. Big Brother continued undeterred even when Karol Wojtyla returned to Poland as Pope.

✦   ✦   ✦

Even then, the Holy Father took the same precautions as before. For example, when he met with opposition leaders in Warsaw, he invited his interlocutors to talk in the garden of the primate's residence, where he was staying at the time.

Prior to the 1983 trip to Poland, there were long negotiations about whether John Paul II would be allowed to meet the ex-leader of Solidarity, Lech Walesa. General Jaruzelski finally gave his okay, so they chose a lodge on the slopes of the Tatras, where they prepared a splendid room, all nicely furnished and well lighted.

The Holy Father went in and looked around, but he obviously felt that something wasn't quite right. He took Walesa's arm and led him outside into the corridor, where they talked, safe from eavesdroppers.

8.

Dissent Explodes

After ten years in prison and eight years of forced labor, Cardinal Stefan Trochta's martyrdom was finally over. But not even in death was he accorded a minimum of respect by the Czechoslovak regime. In April 1974, Wojtyla went to Litomerice with two other cardinals, König and Bengsch, but he was refused permission to concelebrate the funeral Mass. Nevertheless, at the end of the service, he took the opportunity to commemorate Trochta's heroism, despite the presence of the secret police surrounding the church.

Immediately following World War II the Czechoslovak Church was practically destroyed, virtually wiped out. Members of religious orders were deported. A lot of priests were arrested, shot, or were never heard from again. Bishops were sentenced to penal servitude and ended up in the Gulag. But now, the first timid signals were beginning to emerge from the catacombs where Catholics had been forced to live.

They asked for everything, especially Bibles and books and manuals for priestly formation. And after a while, since they weren't allowed to perform ordinations at home, they begged the bishops of the neighboring countries to ordain their seminarians, who would then return to Czechoslovakia to carry out their ministry. And Cardinal Wojtyla, who was already helping them, immediately offered his services.

You mustn't forget that all of this was being done in the most absolute secrecy. If the Communist authorities had gotten the least whiff of anything, they would have immediately broken the chain of solidarity.

At night, the seminarians would bravely set out on their risky journey across the border. On the other side, there would be someone waiting to take them to Kraków. The next step after that was the "recognition." Every young man had half of the certificate authorizing his ordination, and it had to match up with the other half, which the archbishop would have received in the meantime. Finally, there was the ordination ceremony in the cardinal's private chapel, which would obviously be performed with the utmost discretion. The cardinal would lay hands on the young men and make them ministers of Christ. And then, as soon as it was dark, they would begin the journey home—without knowing what to expect when they got there.

At that point, it was still difficult to read the signs of the times. Czechoslovakia had always been the most closed of the Soviet Empire's satellites. And the country had watched its dreams collapse as the tank tracks crushed the half-open flowers of what was called the "Prague Spring." And yet, even the Czechoslovakian fortress began to show a few cracks when—with an uncanny timing suggestive of common frustrations—dissent broke out simultaneously more or less everywhere in Eastern Europe.

In all probability, the movement originated with the signing of the Helsinki Accords on August 1, 1975. The accords appeared to ratify the "logic" of Yalta and the "inviolability" of the borders imposed by Stalin's fiat after World War II. The truth, however, was that (thanks in part to the action of the Holy See) important principles regarding respect for human rights and basic liberties—including freedom of religion—had been quietly slipped into the documents. And that, in turn, gave the dissident groups a solid anchor to rely on.

Thus, although the division of Europe continued in the background, there were foreshadowings of a scenario that was in certain respects new, or at least no longer so rigid.

That's exactly why Cardinal Wojtyla was doubly convinced that the future of the world, and of Poland in particular, couldn't possibly belong to Marxism. The desire for freedom, democracy, and solidarity that he felt arising from the citizenry was just too strong. By the same token, Wojtyla—like the primate, who had the same reaction—was rather pained to see the direction Vatican policy was then moving in vis-à-vis the Communist East. In other words, he was afraid that instead of concerted action with the local episcopates, there was a tendency to make a separate peace with each government—out of a desire, which was legitimate and understandable in itself, to "salvage what could be salvaged."

In addition to everything else, Poland was a pretty atypical case in the Communist archipelago. For one thing, it had a strong, united, and well-organized Church. But its dissent was also different from that of the other Eastern countries.

In countries like East Germany and Czechoslovakia, or like Bulgaria, Hungary, and Russia, dissent was restricted to an in-

tellectual elite, or to revisionist politicians, or to members of small religious groups. On the shores of the Vistula, everything was different. The phenomenon had grown into a mass movement representing the entire nation.

The judgment of Polish society was unanimous: Not only was the Communist system inefficient and incapable of raising the people's standard of living to a minimum level of decency but it was above all unjust and deeply, deeply discriminatory.

If you didn't belong to the Party, you couldn't—with rare exceptions—be a director of anything. Only Party members, then, enjoyed privileges, whereas the Church and its members, its believing and practicing laymen, were treated like second-class citizens.

Wojtyla had been making the same point for years in the language of the Church's social teaching. Obviously, this teaching didn't agree with Marxist ideology, and so it was liquidated under the rubric of political interference.

This brings us to June 25, 1976, a day that would change the history of Poland forever.

There were protests that day in Radom, a small city not far from Warsaw, and at the Ursus tractor factory on the outskirts of the city. The reason for the demonstrations was an all too familiar one: the latest increase in the price of staple commodities. What was new about June 25, though, was that for the first time intellectuals, students, and farmers joined with the workers who faced police harassment because they were marching for their rights. This was the birth of KOR (Komitet Obrony Robotników), an organization dedicated to defending incarcerated workers and their families. The founders of KOR belonged to different schools of thought. Some were Catholics and some weren't. This showed that people were beginning to cross ideological bound-aries and set aside entrenched prejudices in the name of soli-darity and the common good.

Poland rebelled against the one-party state that had failed to represent it, and the rebellion helped Polish society rediscover its strength and its subjectivity. Meanwhile, the Church used the full weight of its moral authority to support and cement this new unity. Cardinal Wyszynski intervened to ask the government to stop the harassment, the arrests, and the trials. For his part, Cardinal Wojtyla insisted that peace could be built only on the basis of respect for the rights of man and the rights of the nation.

Without entering directly into the conflict, Wojtyla wanted to get out the message that the very nation that had fought so much for its independence, that held democracy in such high esteem, that during World War II had suffered so much on many different fronts in the fight for freedom—that this very nation was being deprived of its fundamental rights and freedoms.

In some sense, Wojtyla's words provided an ethical framework for the events we've been discussing, events that anticipated the revolution Solidarity would bring to Poland just a few years down the road.

9.

Rebel Youth

The first time Polish youth protested was in 1968. The protest begin in Warsaw and spread throughout the entire country. It was a very significant step on the road to freedom, even though it later came to light that the secret police were probably behind the unrest. They were most likely implementing a carefully thought-out strategy: to provoke the student revolt and then unleash a repression that would squash it once and for all in the Communist world.

The reason the 1968 revolution didn't succeed was that the youth weren't supported by the workers, who were the backbone of Poland. In fact, the workers actually pitched in to help the riot police. Doubtless they were being manipulated and dragged to the demonstrations by Party agitators.

The Church, especially Cardinal Wojtyla, aligned itself with the youth. This support sent a very clear message. It was a way of saying that the young people weren't the ones responsible for the conflicts and the protests. Instead, the blame had to be laid at the feet of those who had stripped the young of their freedom

LEWES PUBLIC LIBRARY, INC.
111 ADAMS AVENUE
LEWES, DE 19958

and stolen their hopes of ever seeing any real social and cultural development.

This explains why the Church never lost the young, but actually won them back. And why the young didn't lose hope. They may have surrendered their material weapons, but they held on to their spiritual ones.

Before ten years had passed, the second great youth protest broke out. This time, though, the landscape was very different. If there was a place where the students were safe from manipulation by the regime, it was no longer Warsaw, but Kraków— thanks especially to the presence of a highly placed protector like Wojtyla. In addition, there weren't any more self-professed Communists among the youth, who had by now seen their last illusions go up in the smoke of a "real socialism" that wasn't able to deliver any genuine social progress.

In short, Karol Wojtyla's method had proved to be a winner. Wojtyla didn't oppose the regime head-on, but rather deflated it from the inside, by showing how it differed from the reality of man, from the truth about man himself.

I'd like to go a little deeper with that. Cardinal Wojtyla's method of action flowed purely from the Church and the Gospel. He tried to help the young develop a mature moral conscience. He wanted to aid them in finding the inner freedom that comes from contact with God, from dialogue with Him in prayer.

But then this new inner life, this robust connection with God, leads almost naturally to a deeper grasp of social issues, to solidarity with others, to concern for those who suffer or have been denied their freedom and their basic rights.

The result was a moral and spiritual opposition movement.

But it was a by-product of something else, and in any case, its leader was not Karol Wojtyla, who was always a pastor, never a political agitator. He restricted himself to proclaiming the truth. He followed the Gospel principle that "the truth will make you free," and so by the very fact of proclaiming the truth, he also proclaimed man's freedom. It was others who went on to draw the practical conclusions from his principles.

On May 7, 1977, the corpse of a young college student was discovered on a stairway landing in Kraków. It was the body of Stanislaw Pyjas, an organizer for KOR. He was riddled with wounds, and there was blood everywhere. Clearly, the police account of his death, which claimed that he had "fallen down the stairs roaring drunk," was a fabrication.

As soon as I heard about Pyjas's death, I rushed to the gate of the building where the crime had been committed. For that is what it was: a crime. Everyone knows now that it was an assassination—carried out against one of the main organizers of the opposition in Kraków. But at the time, the regime, or whoever had made the decision in the regime, obviously didn't want to admit it.

I stayed there for a few hours, and that was already enough to get me into trouble. All the way back to Franciszkańska Street, I was shadowed and watched by the secret police.

When I got to the residence, I found Wojtyla with the primate, who had come for a procession in honor of Saint Stanislas, whose feast was the next day. I told them what had happened and both of them were extremely upset. They couldn't believe that the regime would go so far as to assassinate someone simply for being linked with the opposition—simply for being inconvenient.

There was a sudden outburst of collective indignation. The students proclaimed three days of mourning. They organized a requiem Mass and an evening procession to Stanislaw's house. Tension ran extraordinarily high. Some even feared the outbreak of civil war. This wasn't so far-fetched, because Kraków was literally invaded by military detachments from all over Poland. Fortunately, Wyszynski and Wojtyla, while speaking the truth, didn't push anyone over the edge, but managed to avoid the worst, to prevent actual fighting and bloodshed.

The primate resolutely proclaimed his support for the young people and condemned the crime that had been committed. At the same time, though, he warned them against resorting to violence. At the first solemn gathering, Wojtyla, speaking to a crowd of thousands of young people, insistently called upon the authorities to respect human rights.

The archbishop thought that the battle had to be fought peacefully and prudently, in the same way that Gandhi had fought his. He thought the first thing you had to rely on was reason, and that you had to find suitable arguments and point out the mistakes of the system. That was the way to prevent the regime from ignoring—or, even worse, trampling—the rights of man, the right to freedom. He didn't want people to think that they could solve problems by stirring up unrest or even an armed uprising.

As he was talking, an airplane flew over the heads of the crowd. The intention was obviously to harass those assembled there.

Wojtyla offered an ironic salute to this "unwelcome guest" and then attacked the press for falsifying the truth. The cardinal's words turned out to be prophetic: The next day, his statements were completely ignored by the newspapers.

None of this did any good, however. The regime was too much a prisoner of its own ideological mechanisms and its own absolute rigidity to notice the threat hanging over its head. Rather, it reacted with the same old methods: repression, lies, and the censor's scissors. As for the censorship, it was the same as always. It was very harsh and rigid, of course, but it could also make itself ridiculous by taking pickiness to new heights of absurdity.

It wasn't just what was said that got censored, but even the individual words that were used. For example, the word *nation* wasn't allowed, much less any criticism of the Communist system or any positive remark about what the Church was doing. They didn't let a single thing slip through. And you had to fight endless battles to secure uncut publication of texts like the documents of the Apostolic See. They even tried to censor the Popes.

This was the Poland that held the reins of power: a Poland that was an absolute minority, without any following among the young, who had by now repudiated the hopelessly authoritarian and oppressive Communist system. And then there was the other Poland, which could claim the majority of the population as its own: the Poland of the "flying universities," whose curriculum offered an alternative to the academic agenda imposed by the state; the Poland where the Church continued to gain credibility, not only among the peasants in the countryside but also among the working class, the bourgeoisie, and the leading representatives of culture.

And Cardinal Wojtyla spoke openly of this "new" Poland at the shrine of Kalwaria Zebrzydowska in 1978: "Something completely new is being born. I would call it a spontaneous, passionate search for the 'faithful witness.' Jesus is this witness. That is why contemporary man is turning to Him. Above all it is today's youth who are turning to Him, because they realize that the fight for the presence or absence of God in the life of man, of the whole people, and of the whole nation calls for a particular encounter with Christ."

10.

"A Slav Will Be Pope"

It was 1978, a year that would be called "the year of three Popes."

Surely, Karol Wojtyla could never have imagined, on that first Sunday of August, what would happen within just a couple of months.

He was vacationing with friends in Bieszczady when he heard the news that Pope Paul VI had died. It was well known that the Pope had been sick, very sick, in fact. But when Wojtyla found out that Paul VI had passed away, he was deeply grieved. He had a close connection with the Pope, whom he looked on as a father. And right from the beginning, Wojtyla had been favorably impressed by Paul VI's pastoral style, his way of looking at the world, and the huge openness he always showed to the problems of the culture.

The Church started preparing for the conclave.

Many observers predicted a tough, complicated election, both because there were now more cardinals and because the con-

flicts dividing the Church in the long and tumultuous postconciliar period were far from over.

Cardinal Wojtyla never speculated about who would succeed Pope Paul. He would merely say, "The Holy Spirit will show us whom He wants." He looked at everything with the eyes of faith, with the eyes of a believer, of a man of the Church.

In Rome, he also met up again with Albino Luciani, the patriarch of Venice. They didn't know each other well, but they had met frequently and there was a great spiritual affinity between them.

I remember one of those meetings, which took place at the Pontifical Polish College in Piazza Remuria. The conclave was in preparation. Cardinal Wojtyla invited the patriarch to lunch, and the patriarch gladly accepted. I got a chance to meet him, too, and I immediately liked him because of his spontaneity.

Another interesting meeting was with Cardinal Joseph Ratzinger. I think that they talked about the Church's need to offer a specifically Catholic and Christian proposal to the contemporary world on the eve of the millennium.

Contrary to predictions, the conclave came to a speedy conclusion. The election went extraordinarily quickly, a sign that the College of Cardinals had found unity at a decisive moment in Church history. Perhaps it was precisely to reinforce this cohesion that Luciani took a double name—John Paul—that united the legacies of his two immediate predecessors. And that reconciled the different (though not, as was often wrongly believed, contrary) approaches identified with these two previous Popes.

◆   ◆   ◆

Cardinal Wojtyla never recounted the details of the conclave. All he said was that you could feel the presence of the Holy Spirit at work during the proceedings. He accepted the new Pope's election as the will of God. He was confident God had made His choice known to the cardinals.

He met with John Paul I immediately after the inauguration of his pontificate. Then he left for Kraków. He liked to recall the Pope's kind, joyful smile, which was an expression of his deep faith.

A mere thirty-three days went by.

Wojtyla had recently returned from a visit to West Germany with a delegation of the Polish bishops headed up by Cardinal Wyszynski. Since being back in Poland, he had visited the shrine of Kalwaria and had celebrated a solemn Mass in the Wawel Cathedral to honor Saint Wenceslas and to mark the twentieth anniversary of his episcopal ordination.

On the morning of September 29, Wojtyla was sitting over his tea, when his driver, Mucha, suddenly rushed into the room. Red in the face from agitation, Mucha barely managed to break the news: John Paul I was dead.

The archbishop stiffened, but only for a second. He interrupted breakfast and retired to his apartment. He wanted to be alone at that sad moment. He didn't say anything; we only heard him whispering, "This is unbelievable . . . unbelievable." From the other end of the hall, we saw him going into the chapel. And he stayed there for a long time, praying.

Praying. And maybe asking himself, asking God, why this had happened. He asked the same question at the funeral Mass in the Mariacka Basilica, where he opened his heart and said, "The whole world, the whole Church, is asking, Why? . . . We do not know what this death means for the See of Peter. We do not know what Christ is trying to tell the Church and the world through this event."

At the Vatican, it was almost like a replay of the scenes of August. For Wojtyla, though, everything was different.

Even privately, he never talked about who would succeed Pope John Paul I.

Inwardly, though, he was not at peace, and those who knew him could read it on his face. Perhaps he was uneasy because he had learned that no less influential a cardinal than Franz König often mentioned him as a papabile at meetings with fellow members of the Sacred College.

The evening before the beginning of the conclave, he went to greet the priests of the Polish College, where he used to lodge when he went to Rome. His greeting was intense and brotherly, but there wasn't a single person who didn't notice how tense he was or how preoccupied he looked.

The next morning, I accompanied the cardinal to the Vatican. Before that, though, we went to the Gemelli Clinic to visit Bishop (today Cardinal) Andrzej Maria Deskur, who had suffered a stroke just a few days earlier and was now in intensive care. He was in critical condition, and he hadn't yet regained consciousness.

Years later, Karol Wojtyla, now Pope, would recall Bishop Deskur's sudden illness and say that he had read it as a sign, which had gotten him worrying. You see, this wasn't the first time in his life that he had received a sign like that. For example, when he was about to be ordained bishop, he asked one of his dearest friends, Cardinal Marian Jaworski (who is today the Latin-rite archbishop of Lviv), to take his place preaching at a retreat for a group of priests. Jaworski set off, but there was a dreadful train wreck, in which he lost one of his arms. And then, on the very eve of the conclave, Deskur's stroke. So the Pope's point was that he felt that his election was somehow connected with his friend's suffering.

And with that, we come to the conclave itself.

What happened behind closed doors there is a secret sealed by an oath. We don't know any of the details. So let's just leave it at the Holy Spirit and the wisdom of the Church.

Okay. No one wants to guess, much less to speculate, here. And yet, proceeding with due caution, and basing our assumptions on a few authoritative voices, we can attempt a very minimal reconstruction of what happened at the conclave. At least for the sake of understanding the background behind Wojtyla's election as well as the steps leading up to it.

Well, then, the conclave began on October 14, 1978. The whole next day was a contest between supporters of Giuseppe Siri, the archbishop of Genoa, and backers of Giovanni Benelli, the archbishop of Florence. Both were Italians, but they stood for divergent positions. Siri maintained the need for a certain course correction in relation to the route the Church had taken after Vatican II. Benelli, by contrast, favored pushing ahead with the implementation of Vatican II while maintaining full fidelity to the spirit and letter of the council's teaching. The two candidates were passed over. Better: They canceled each other out.

The following day, October 16, began with two rounds of vot-

ing, in which Wojtyla garnered a certain amount of support. Then, according to the account given by Cardinal Luigi Ciappi, the turning point came during the afternoon break, when Wojtyla's backers gradually won over the other cardinals.

König was almost certainly the one who engineered this gradual shift in the consensus. He had already spoken with Wyszynski and convinced him that Wojtyla would be a good choice (at first, Wyszynski mistakenly thought König was proposing him, Wyszynski). The primate then went to Wojtyla's room to comfort and encourage him—and to urge him to accept.

He repeated to Wojtyla the question at the heart of Sienkiewicz's novel Quo Vadis?, which occurs when Jesus encounters Peter as the apostle tries to slip out of Rome. But then he softened his tone and begged Wojtyla not to refuse if he should be elected. And he added, "The new Pope's task will be to lead the Church into the third millennium."

Wojtyla returned to the Sistine Chapel looking more relaxed, although his heart was in tumult. An old friend of his, Cardinal Maximilian de Furstenberg, who had been his rector at the Belgian College, came up to him and whispered into his ear a line from the ordination service for priests: "Deus adest et vocat te," or "God is here and he is calling you."

In the eighth round of voting, the second of that afternoon, Wojtyla was elected—apparently—with ninety-nine votes. He was deeply affected, but he had regained his serenity. He accepted, choosing the same name as Luciani had.

I later found out from Cardinal Wyszynski that he, Wyszynski, had always urged him to take that name, in memory of the deceased Pope and out of respect for the Italian people, who had dearly loved John Paul I.

✦   ✦   ✦

All of the cardinals approached the Pope-elect to pay their re-
spect. When Wojtyla saw Wyszynski coming toward him, he
opened his arms and enfolded him in a long embrace.

Meanwhile, the white smoke was rising from the chimney of
the Sistine Chapel.

A century earlier, the great poet Juliusz Slowacki had written,
"And so a Slav will be Pope, a brother of the peoples."

I was standing in Saint Peter's Square, near the gate of the basilica. That's where I heard Cardinal Pericle Felici announce the
name of the new Pope: It was my bishop! My bishop!

Of course I was exultant, but I felt sort of paralyzed, as if I'd
been turned into stone. I thought to myself, It's happened! It
wasn't supposed to happen, but it has just happened. In Kraków
there were people who were praying that he wouldn't be elected,
because they didn't want him to leave, but to stay in the diocese.
No one thought that anything like this could happen. But it did!
It had just happened!

In Poland, too, there was an initial moment of disbelief, though
it was soon followed by an outburst of joy. Poles poured into the
streets and the squares to shout out their happiness and excite-
ment, not to mention all their pride in seeing one of their own
ascend the throne of Peter.

Someone managed to recognize me in the midst of the crowd.
They came and took me to the conclave, though it was still
closed.

＊　＊　＊

In the Vatican, the Pope was putting on his new papal cassock. He was supposed to appear on the balcony of Saint Peter's and bless the people gathered in the square. As he approached the balcony and saw the huge crowd below, he asked the person accompanying him if he shouldn't perhaps say a few words. His companion answered in the negative: It wasn't part of the usual ritual. But when he reached the balcony, John Paul II felt a sort of irresistible inner command.

"Praised be Jesus Christ," he said. The people answered: "Both now and forever." Then he began to speak.

"I don't know if I can manage to say what I want to say in your—in our Italian language. If I make a mistake, you will correct me." This was followed by a burst of applause that seemed like it would never end.

The doors of the conclave finally opened and the marshal, Marchese Giulio Sacchetti, led me inside the Vatican. The Holy Father was already dining with all the cardinals. When I came in, the cardinal chamberlain, Jean Villot, stood up and presented me to the new Pope with a smile on his face.

It was a very simple encounter, but for me it was extraordinarily moving. He was looking at me. Maybe he was trying to guess what I felt seeing him dressed as Pope. He didn't say anything, but he spoke to me with his eyes, because he could do that, you know. He could look right into your soul. I was in the presence of the universal shepherd of the Church, the Pope. Then it finally sank in: He was no longer Cardinal Wojtyla, but John Paul II, the successor of Peter.

He leaned toward me and finally broke the silence. All he said to me was half a line, just a couple of words, but they were full of his old humor, and they immediately brought me out of my state of overwhelming emotion and enabled me to recognize the man I had always known. He was clearly referring to the cardinals and wanted to convey to me his surprise that they had elected him. So what he wanted to say was, more or less, "What have they *done*?" But that's my . . . "translation." Actually, what he said to me was a sentence in the Roman dialect, which he purposely abbreviated: *"Li possino . . ."*

I went to eat dinner in another room with the secretary of the conclave, Archbishop Ernesto Civardi, the master of ceremonies, and other people who had helped out in the preceding days. They looked at me with curiosity, but also with goodwill.

After dinner, the Holy Father went back to his room, a little apartment he was sharing with the archbishop of Naples, Corrado Ursi, on the mezzanine of the wing belonging to the secretary of state. He and Ursi knew each other well, since they had been named cardinals together.

And there, in that little room, the new Pope began his first "task." He started preparing his speech for the following day, which he had to read in Latin. But he already knew what he wanted to say, and the writing flowed easily. This would be his inaugural speech, where he would sketch the main lines of his pontificate and the tasks that he would carry out by God's will. Among the key points were the implementation of Vatican II, openness to the world, ecumenism, and the situation of Catholicism at that point in the history of the Church and the world.

After dinner, I went back to the Polish College, and the other priests and I spent the whole night talking about the big event. Meanwhile, we were trying to hear the reactions from Kraków and other Polish cities over the radio. We heard reports of great joy and tears among the people, and we listened to the prayers, the vigils being held in the churches, the Masses, and the sound of the bells ringing. In the Wawel Cathedral, they rang the majestic bell of Sigismund, which they used to do only in exceptional circumstances.

But there were some who weren't rejoicing, who were literally in a state of shock and trauma on account of Wojtyla's election. In Poland, the news was held back from publication, because the Central Party Committee was at a loss as to how to convey it, as to how to mitigate the explosive repercussions it was bound to have. And it wasn't just in Poland that there was such huge dismay. It was all over the Communist world, especially in the Kremlin. For ten days, there was absolute silence in the empire. No statement. No comment.

History had taken sensational revenge on those who thought they could erase God from men's lives.

When Cardinal Wojtyla left for the conclave, the Communist authorities withdrew his diplomatic visa, and issued him only a tourist visa instead. One of the provincial Party secretaries said, "By all means go to Rome. We'll settle things when you get back."

Who knows what must have gone through that zealous bureaucrat's mind when he saw Cardinal Wojtyla return less than a year later dressed in the papal white.

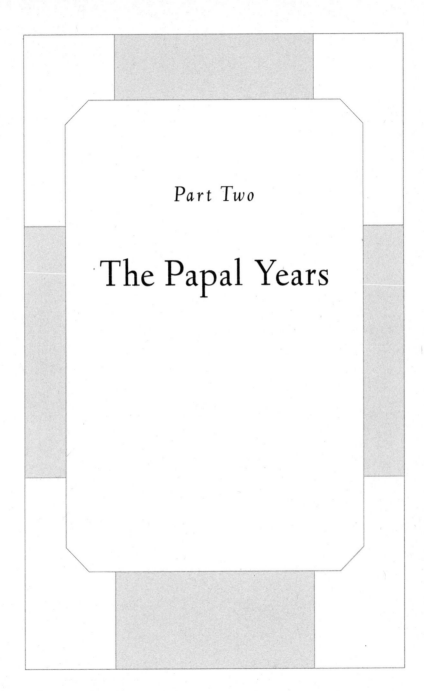

Part Two

The Papal Years

11.

"Open the Doors to Christ"

It was Sunday, October 22, 1978. The new Pope, who happened to be the first Slavic Pontiff in history, was officially inaugurating his papal ministry. In his homily for the installation ceremony, he delivered an unforgettable exhortation: "Be not afraid! Open the doors to Christ, open them wide! Open the borders of states, economic and political systems, the vast domains of culture, civilization, and development—open them to His saving power!"

This appeal wasn't addressed only to Catholics, or even only to Christians. John Paul II knew the world was facing an unprecedented challenge. Man's temptation to refuse God in the name of his own freedom and autonomy had by this point transcended all religious differences to take on planetary proportions.

I was struck by the Pope's homily as soon as I read it. I was struck because it expressed the Holy Father's spirit, thought, and program. It laid out the program of his life, of his heart, of his religious devotion. At the same time, it also set forth the program for the pastoral service he was inaugurating in the Church as the successor of Peter.

So I think that those words—"Be not afraid! Open . . ."—were the motto of his life and the master key to his pontificate. Those words were meant to inspire strength and courage, especially in the nations groaning under the yoke of bondage. To them, his words were a proclamation of freedom.

Among those attending the ceremony in Saint Peter's Square were the Soviet ambassador to Italy and, standing next to him, the president of the Polish Council of State, Henryk Jablonski. At a certain point, the ambassador turned toward his neighbor and whispered in a contemptuous tone, "The greatest feat of the People's Republic of Poland has been to give the world a Pope." He meant a Pope from Eastern Europe, a Pope who was intimately familiar with the Communist world, who knew how to deal with it. And so it was time to start thinking about how to counteract this Pope.

But perhaps the ambassador forgot that the words "Be not afraid!" didn't come to John Paul II from an ideology, or a political strategy, but from the practice of the Gospel and the imitation of Christ. That was his strength! Armed with those words, he set out to travel the ways of the world and, I think, to transform it.

In fact, Karol Wojtyla immediately started on this path. As soon as the solemn inaugural ceremony was finished, he took hold of the pastoral cross, almost as if it were a banner or a flag, and proceeded with a firm step down the length of Saint Peter's Square. It was as if he wanted to go out to meet the whole world, to shake it out of its passivity and resignation, its fears and myths, its illusion of being able to live without God.

Immediately after his election, the Holy Father said that he didn't want the gestatorial chair. It was one of the first things he said, precisely because he wanted to prevent them from offering it to him. He had good legs, a mountaineer's legs, and he preferred to use them.

In the same spirit, he refused the tiara. It wasn't that he was rejecting the symbolic link with a temporal power whose time had passed. No, the point was much simpler: Vatican II had created a more Gospel-oriented, more spiritual Church.

Besides, his predecessor, Pope John Paul I, had also started off on the same note by forgoing the so-called coronation. And Wojtyla liked that pastoral style. He thought it was more suitable to the new times and more in keeping with the mission of the universal shepherd, who has to stay close to the people—better: who has to go among the people.

As John Paul II himself would later confide, it wasn't until afterward that he perceived the full depth of his words in Saint Peter's and realized that they expressed something he had been carrying in his heart and soul for a long time.

The fact of the matter is that he threw that homily together. All alone, by hand, with just a few corrections, and, of course, in Polish. But then, once it was translated into Italian, he wanted to rehearse, so to speak. He read it to Angelo Gugel, the papal butler. And Angelo was very exact and rigorous, and if the Pope made mistakes with the accents, Angelo would correct him.

But it is true. What the Pope said that October Sunday was

part of his memory, his history, and the legacy of faith and culture he had brought from his native land to the chair of Peter.

It's good that you mention that, because it was the source of John Paul II's vision of the relation between the mystery of the Redemption and the truth about man. This vision then became the center of his first encyclical, Redemptor Hominis. "By his Incarnation, he, the Son of God, in a certain way united himself with each man." In other words, Christ gradually reveals to man—to man who is the "primary and fundamental way" of the Church—the core of his very being, his destiny, and his unique and unrepeatable uniqueness as a person in possession of an original dignity of his own.

That's a truth contained in the Gospel, which was then rediscovered and reaffirmed by Vatican II, especially by the Pastoral Constitution *Gaudium et Spes*. The same truth was also the fruit of the reflections, ideas, and experiences that had ripened in Karol Wojtyla during his years as priest, teacher, and bishop. So his programmatic encyclical was the synthesis of Vatican II and the legacy he brought with him from Poland. The Pope then translated this synthesis into a commitment to combine the Church's mission with service to all men—all men, not just abstractly, not just symbolically, but in their concrete, historical reality, both as individuals and as members of social communities.

Perhaps this point wasn't so apparent when Redemptor Hominis came out. There wasn't much talk of it in the newspapers. But the Pope's "option for man" did not go down easily with all ecclesiastics, or with all theologians, for that matter. Some were even scandalized by his claim that man is the "way" of the

Church. It was as if by shifting attention to the centrality of the human subject, the new Pope had detracted from the primacy of God.

We can't forget the words "Be not afraid!" because they inspired John Paul II to make man the central idea of *Redemptor Hominis.* Insofar as he is redeemed by Christ, man is the "way" of the Church. The Pope was talking about the whole man, body and soul, who lives in a constant tension between freedom and truth.

Yes, perhaps you're right. At least in some circles, at least at that point, when the Church was still feeling the weight of certain fears, those words may have come as a shock or caused people to turn up their noses. But then they became the program of the whole Church and the pontificate. The program is still just as relevant today as it was then. It's an integral part of the Magisterium and of the mission of the Church community.

In a word, what at the time looked quasi-heretical to some was actually a big factor in overcoming the old opposition between theocentrism and anthropocentrism. The encyclical linked them precisely in man's historical existence. It thus anticipated what would become the main question of the twenty-first century for both the Church and humanity: the question of man.

What will the man of tomorrow be like? How will his concrete existence look? What values, what ethical reference points, what patterns and styles of life will he adopt? And so, how can we possibly understand, much less solve, the question of man if we ignore the question of God?

12.

A Journey to
Anticlerical Mexico

One day, the new Pope found a letter on his desk. It was an invitation to visit Puebla, Mexico, for the third general conference of the Latin American episcopate.

It wasn't easy for him to decide whether or not to accept.

Back then, in 1979, Mexico was still an officially anticlerical country. There were a lot of Masons in government, in parliament, and in the upper echelons of business. In addition, if he wanted to set foot on Mexican soil, the head of the Catholic Church would have to request a visa, and he would not be allowed to bless the faithful in the open air or in the streets.

The main preoccupation, though, was how to deal with the issue of liberation theology. In the beginning, liberation theology did express something deep in the soul of Latin American Catholicism. But then it became contaminated by radical schools of thought that distorted both pastoral practice and Church teaching. The result was an identification of the mission to evangelize with revolutionary action.

A final factor that had to be weighed was the then-current

domination of Latin America by so-called national security regimes, which opposed Marxism and presented a facade of Christianity, but in reality only perpetuated the suppression of human rights and freedom.

Certain voices urged caution, or at least a deferment of the trip. But the Holy Father decided to accept the invitation. He said, "The episcopate has invited me and I can't not go. I have to join the bishops in pondering the dramatic problems facing Latin America, starting with liberation theology. Because we have to wonder: Where is this theology headed? Is it going to result in Marxist class struggle, or will it lead to Christian liberation, which is about love, solidarity, and the fundamental option for the poor?"

And then the Holy Father added another argument: "If they receive me in an anticlerical country like Mexico now, how can they refuse to allow me to return to Poland later?"

So the new Pope's first trip outside of Italy was to Mexico. And it was a good thing, too. First of all, it awakened an extraordinary response among Mexican Catholics, whom it allowed to emerge at last from a long and painful minority status. But another reason was that the Mexico trip gave John Paul II a chance to become personally acquainted with the Latin American scene, and so to learn the language of liberation and to discover the most genuine interpretations of it—to such an extent, in fact, that his experience in Mexico gave birth to two of the main social ideas of his pontificate.

Everything began, then, with an amazing celebration that burst out when the Pope set foot in Mexico City. Huge crowds poured into the streets. The chant that later became famous throughout the world also made its debut: "Juan Pablo Segundo, te quiere todo el mundo" (John Paul II, the whole world loves you). Happily surprised, Karol Wojtyla abandoned himself to what was an almost-smothering embrace. And, infected by the contagious spontaneity of the people, he started improvising, dialoguing with his audience, and not in his mother tongue.

They had scheduled a meeting at the Miguel Ángel Institute in Mexico City with students from the Catholic schools. Well, tens of thousands of kids showed up. When he saw the throng of people, the Holy Father quickly scanned the text he was supposed to read and realized that it was no longer suited for his audience. He didn't feel confident in Spanish, either, since he had started studying it again only a couple of months earlier. He said to Santos Abril, who worked for the Secretariat of State, "I'll talk in Italian and you translate." But then the young people were so enthusiastic that he started speaking directly in Spanish. And his talk is still remembered there today.

The main event, of course, was the Pope's speech in Puebla before the entire Latin American episcopate. The Pope was tough in reasserting Catholic doctrine about Christ (He is not the "'subversive of Nazareth'") and the Church (it cannot be reduced to a platform for socio-political praxis emerging from the people). But he was extremely open on the social front: "The Church has to keep its freedom with respect to the opposing systems, so that its only option is for man."

His words—and the bishops, and many of the theologians, were the first to think so—were important and, in certain respects, arguably new, as well. The Holy Father defended the dignity of the

Church and its independence from political and economic systems and governments. He wasn't pushing a simple moral equivalence, or trying to present some "third way," between the ideologies of Marxism and liberalism. His point was that the Church, basing itself on the Gospel, claimed the right to judge whether or not the various political programs were compatible with God's plan for humanity.

In other words, the Church wanted to remain at man's service; it desired man's freedom from every sort of coercion, abuse of power, and injustice; it wanted to secure his freedom to profess his faith in God. That's what the Pope was doing: exercising an "option for man."

All of this came up again in Oaxaca and Monterrey. In Cuilapan, in the state of Oaxaca, the Pope met with the indios and the campesinos. The evening before the meeting, he read the greeting prepared by the spokesman of the indigenous community, who spoke out against those guilty of depriving numerous families of their daily bread. The Pope reinforced the accusation in his own speech the following day: "It is not just, it is not human, it is not Christian." The speech he gave in Monterrey, a stop that was only decided upon in Mexico City, was written at the last minute. And, speaking before the workers, the Pope had hard words for the industry barons who exploited their employees and he denounced the economic policies of the government.

Well, the journalists and pundits used those two speeches to insinuate an opposition between the "Third World Pope" of Cuilapan and Monterrey and the "integralist" Pope of Puebla. And, more generally, to present the Mexico trip as the beginning of a restorationist shift, of a Polonization of the universal Church.

◆ ◆ ◆

Let me say right off that neither then nor afterward did the Holy Father ever let himself be governed by the criticisms he received, much less by biased and manipulative ones like those. He got everything from prayer, from the encounter with the Lord. And because he followed the Gospel, he also knew which road to take and which direction to lead the Church, and he forged straight ahead, without looking either to the right or to the left. He always imitated Christ and tried to be the good shepherd of the flock. He was a free man. He was interiorly free, and that gave him serenity.

Conservative? Traditionalist?

Those criticisms assumed that a Pope who came from Poland couldn't be anything but that. What a silly simplification! What a biased and offensive judgment! Remember that at the time something you might call a "superiority complex" was rampant in certain parts of the Western world. In other words, there were people who thought that nothing good could come from the East; people from the East were second-class citizens.

Conservative? Traditionalist? But what does that mean?

John Paul II was a traditionalist on the issues that had to be presented in a traditional way. Tradition is very important in the Church. We have two sources of Revelation: Holy Scripture and tradition. Plus there's theological tradition, as well as national traditions, culture, the Church. A nation without roots would wither like an uprooted tree. And it's true that the Holy Father did what he could to nurture and defend the roots of Christian Europe.

Conservative? Traditionalist?

You'd have to say the same thing about him on the moral front. Karol Wojtyla was very modern about morality. That was nothing new for him. Take his first book, *Love and Responsibility,* where he sets forth a personalist conception of love and fearlessly deals with sexual issues like the mutual giving of sexual pleasure in marriage, shame over the naked body, or female frigidity, which is often a consequence of male egoism. And he wrote about all this in a way that was certainly bold coming from a bishop and at any rate was new, given the scholarship of the time.

And he continued to be very modern as Pope. He was modern in how he argued, how he dealt with questions, and especially in how he looked at the Church's social teaching with new eyes. He was a progressive where he needed to be; and where necessary, he remained a traditionalist in the right sense of the word.

This explains why he was a Pope who never took for granted any of the so-called truths that dominated the world at that particular stage of history. For example, the "truth" that contemporary man was on an inevitable course toward a future cut loose from any sort of spiritual dimension; and that the final outcome of secularization would necessarily be the disappearance of religion, or at least its relegation to a marginal status in the sacristies and in the consciences of believers; and that the younger generations had therefore left the Church behind once and for all. Another example: John Paul II never took it for granted that Europe had to remain forever divided in two or abandon its tradition of unity, which had sprung up precisely on the soil of Christian faith.

And this same countercultural attitude of his may also explain why the Pope very quickly began to reshuffle the cards, whether in politics and international diplomacy or in a religious world still full of so much division.

13.

A Typical Day in the Life of a Pope

What is a Pope's life in the Vatican like? What does his day look like? Is he able to make room for prayer with all the work he has to do? Is he able to carve out for himself a zone of privacy, despite the inevitably public nature of the responsibilities that come with his job as head of the universal Church?

Obviously, since I lived with John Paul II, I'll be talking about him here. But perhaps I can take the liberty of enlarging the focus for a moment, at least to include the last couple of pontificates. Of course, the Vatican, by virtue of its structure, necessarily makes rules and so imposes a certain conformity of behavior—even on the Pontiffs. I'd like to say, though, that every Pope has managed to use his personality and his gifts to turn the situation upside down. In other words, he has been able to make the big Vatican "machine" follow the rhythms not only of his own spiritual life but also of his human lifestyle, if I may put it like that.

I can tell you from personal observation that Karol Wojtyla was certainly able to pull this off. At the beginning, of course, he inevitably felt a certain nostalgia for the days when he had more freedom and was less strictly bound by protocol. But then he very quickly adapted himself to his new role, to the point that someone might have asked—I'm joking, of course—where he had gone to "Pope school." And, at the same time, he adopted a mode of living—even in the Vatican and even as Pope—that wasn't so different from how he had always lived.

Now, seeing as how I've already hinted at them, I'll start with the excursions the Holy Father would take in the early days, when he was still having a bit of trouble getting adjusted. The problem for him was not so much being cooped up in the Vatican as it was having to stay there for long periods of time.

Just to make myself clear, I'd like to point out that the excursions outside Rome, especially the ones in the mountains, were opportunities—"gifts" was how he put it—for him to meditate and, above all, to pray. The scenery was congenial to his spirituality. In the mountains, he contemplated the works of God and abandoned himself into the hands of their Creator. Obviously, we would chat at meals. But, as soon as we'd finished eating, he would go off walking alone, sometimes for hours, so that he could speak personally with the Lord, as he put it. In short, it was as if the excursions were a chance for him to recharge his batteries. He would even manage to find time to read and prepare magisterial documents.

There were more than a hundred of these expeditions, mostly in Abruzzo. And at the beginning, no one in the Vatican or in the press knew anything about them.

The first time was almost like making an escape. For a long time, we'd wanted to give the Holy Father the chance not only to ski but also to immerse himself again in the normal life of the people. Finally, we decided to give it a shot. I don't remember who originally came up with the idea, but it was probably a collective initiative that emerged from conversation at table. That said, the place we picked, Ovindoli, was suggested by Father Tadeusz Rakoczy (today bishop of Bielsko-Zywiec in Poland), who knew the territory because he used to go skiing in the area. But, just to be safe, he and Father Jozef Kowalczyk (now apostolic nuncio in Poland) went to scope the place out to make sure there would be no surprises.

If memory serves, it was January 2, 1981. We left around 9:00 A.M. in Father Jozef's car, so as not to attract the attention of the Swiss Guards stationed at the exit of the residence at Castel Gandolfo. Father Jozef was the driver and Father Tadeusz sat in the passenger's seat, pretending to read the newspaper, which he held completely open so as to shield from view the Holy Father, who was sitting in back next to me.

Father Jozef drove with extreme caution. He obeyed all the speed limits and slowed down at every crosswalk. Imagine what would have happened if there had been an accident or if the car had broken down!

We drove through a lot of villages so that the Pope could enjoy himself looking out the windows and seeing a bit of ordinary life. When we arrived, we parked near one of the ski runs outside of Ovindoli, but there was hardly anyone there. That was the beginning of a wonderful, unforgettable day. Mountains on every side. The landscape completely covered in white. A huge silence in which you could focus your mind and pray. The Holy Father even managed to ski. He was delighted by the "present" we had given him. On the way home, he smiled and said to us, "Well, we did it after all!" And over the next few days he kept on thanking us and recalling the highlights of our outing.

We always tried to choose solitary places for subsequent excursions. But we also had a list of particular ski runs we wanted to visit, which meant that it wasn't always possible to avoid people. But then, why worry about it? The Holy Father acted like a totally normal skier. He was dressed like everyone else: parka, cap, goggles. He stood in line along with everyone else—though we were always clever enough to make sure he was standing between two of our party—and he had a lift ticket that he reused after each run.

You won't believe it, but no one recognized him. After all, who could imagine that a Pope would go *skiing*? One of the first people to discover him was a little boy who couldn't have been more than ten at the time.

It was late afternoon. Father Jozef and I had gone on ahead. Father Tadeusz had just finished a downhill run and was waiting on the slope for the Holy Father. At that point, a little farther down, a group of cross-country skiers passed by. Not long after that, a little boy appeared. He was panting for breath and obviously trying to catch up with the group that had just passed by. He asked Father Tadeusz, "Did you see where they went?" And then, as Father Tadeusz was pointing out which way they'd gone, the kid turned . . . and saw the Holy Father, who had just pulled up. The kid stood for a second staring, his mouth wide open, and then he started bellowing, "The Pope, the Pope!" Father Tadeusz said, "Don't be silly! Better scram, or else you'll never find your friends." The kid went off after the others, while we made our way to the bottom of the hill, got ourselves into the car as quickly as we could, and hurried back to Rome.

Afterward, when people found out that the Pope went skiing and that they could meet him on the slopes, we decided it was better if we were officially escorted by the fire department (so, instead of the car, we started using a van, also because Angelo

Gugel, the papal butler, had joined the party) and by a police vehicle from the Vatican precinct (so as to reassure the Italian authorities). Even so, we still always tried to go to the less crowded
spots. Sometimes we stayed in the mountains until late in the
evening. We would light a fire, fix something to eat, chat, and
then sing together.

But now, it's really time to return to the Vatican and say something about the Pope's daily schedule. The first thing to remember is that John Paul II was a perfectionist, because he always
wanted to get as much as he could out of the time available. So
he would meticulously plan out the day's activities: prayer, work,
meetings, meals (which gave him a chance to talk with guests),
and rest.

Another thing I need to mention is how simply Karol Wojtyla
lived in the Vatican. His personal apartment consisted essentially of a bedroom and a tiny study with a little desk and a chair.
The study was divided from the bedroom by a screen. It was all
very simple. In fact, it was quite Spartan—perfect for a person
like the Pope, who never gave any thought to comfort.

In the Vatican, he continued to live as modestly as he had
lived in Kraków. Truth be told, I have to say that he actually practiced poverty to a heroic degree, but—and this was the most
amazing thing about it—he did it effortlessly. He didn't have anything and he never asked for anything, either. Apart from the fact
that he was no financial whiz and didn't receive any stipend from
the Apostolic See, the Secretariat of State took care of the ex-
penses incurred by his activities. In other words, as Pope his
needs were provided for but he never had a cent to call his own.

Anyway, the Holy Father used to begin his day pretty early. He
would get up at 5:30, wash up, and go to the chapel for morning
adoration, Lauds, and meditation. Mass would be at 7:00 A.M.,

and there was always someone in attendance: laypeople, or priests, or groups of bishops, especially bishops on an *ad limina* visit from this or that country.

When the guests came in (there were never more than fifty), they often found the Pope kneeling in prayer with his eyes closed, in a state of total abandonment, almost of ecstasy, completely unaware of who was entering the chapel. More than one person said that "he looked like he was speaking with the Invisible."

Bishops and priests could concelebrate if they wished. For the laypeople, it was a great spiritual experience. The Holy Father attached extreme importance to the presence of the lay faithful. After all, when everyone was gathered with Christ's Vicar around the eucharistic Lord in a communion of faith, it was as if the whole universal Church were present. It was as if all of humanity, and all its hopes and sorrows, were there.

And the truth is that men and women suffering all over the world were always spiritually present in the chapel. In fact, they were literally close to the Pope's heart, because the little drawer of his prie-dieu was always full of the prayer requests he used to receive. There were letters from AIDS and cancer patients; from a mother requesting prayers for her seventeen-year-old son, who was in a coma. There were also letters from families in crisis. A lot of childless couples would send in requests as well, and they would also write back to thank him when their prayers were answered.

After breakfast, John Paul II would move into his study. He would write notes, homilies, or outlines for speeches. After his shoulder injury, he started dictating, first to me, of course, and subsequently to Father Pawel after he took over the job. The secretary would write down the Pope's words on a laptop and then translate the text into Italian. When he had finished dictating, the Pope would often ask whoever was helping him, "What do you think?" But even the time he set aside for work was peppered with prayers, with short bursts of prayer. So it was as if he never stopped praying throughout the day. It wasn't a rare occurrence for one of the secretaries to look for him and find him prostrate on the floor of the chapel, completely immersed in prayer. Sometimes he would sing quietly during morning adoration, as well.

The private and public visits began each morning at eleven, except for Wednesdays, when he had the general audience. The visitors might be bishops, heads of state, cultural leaders, or dignitaries from this or that country. At the beginning of the pontificate, these audiences would sometimes go on until two-thirty. The Pope never dismissed anyone or interrupted a conversation, but always let his interlocutor say everything that was on his mind. But as time went on, it became necessary to reduce the length of these meetings.

The next item on the agenda was lunch. John Paul II always had guests at table who could inform him directly about what was going on in the world and in the Christian communities. The guests might be the heads of some Vatican dicastery who would fill him in about the work their particular office was doing. And when the Pope had to plan a trip or prepare a document, he would invite the people involved in that particular undertaking.

For the most part, the Pope listened or asked questions, because he wanted to learn about whatever situation or problem was being discussed. He used to eat at a rectangular table. He would always sit on one of the two long sides, with his back to the kitchen door. If there were only just a couple of guests, they would sit facing him; if there were a lot of guests, some would also sit at the shorter sides, where his private secretaries would normally eat.

As time went on, I was joined by other secretaries: Father Emery Kabongo, who came from Zaire; Father Vincent Trân Ngoc Thu, from Vietnam; and Father Mieczyslaw Mokrzycki ("Miecio," as we called him), who was also Polish. And since I am on the subject already, I'd like to mention the sisters who took care of the papal apartments, the Handmaids of the Sacred Heart of Jesus. The sisters were all Polish: Sister Tobiana, Sister Eufrozyna, Sister Germana, Sister Fernanda, and Sister Matylda.

Generally speaking, we ate *all'italiana*. There was pasta, then meat with a side of vegetables. To drink, there was water and a little red wine. In the evenings, it was mostly soup and fish. It was only on big feast days that Polish cuisine would come back into style. Then the sisters could pull out all the stops: first *barszcz,* a soup made of beets, or at least some kind of soup; then what was known as the *kotlet,* a pork chop with potatoes and greens; and for dessert, either poppy-seed cake or a pie with ricotta cheese.

The Pope would eat a little of everything. He wouldn't take much, but he would try everything. That was his custom, which went back to his youth during the war, when all you could get were frugal meals, and the main concern was trying to get at least a bit of bread and a few potatoes. From that time on, Karol Wojtyla had maintained what we might call a certain detachment from food. One thing he especially liked, though, were sweets, particularly Italian ones. And coffee, too, which he drank in the morning and in the afternoon.

As the years went on, the Holy Father needed a longer rest in the afternoon, after which he would pray again. In fact, as soon as he could get away, he would go out onto the balcony. He did that to the very end of his life, both in the winter (with a black priest's coat on his shoulders) and in the summer. It was his favorite place. He would stop to meditate before different images that were set up there. There was an altar with a statue of Our Lady of Fatima that he especially liked. He always said the entire Rosary, which was his favorite devotion. Every Thursday, he would make a holy hour. On Fridays, he did the Stations of the Cross, no matter where he was. He would even pray the Stations on a plane or in a helicopter, as he did once on the way to Galilee.

Mass, the Breviary, frequent visits to the Blessed Sacrament, plus moments of recollection, devotions, weekly Confession, and religious practices (he continued to keep the full fast even at an advanced age) were also fundamentally important parts of his daily spiritual life, by which I mean his constant intimacy with God. And let me say that there was nothing sanctimonious about any of this. He was in love with God. He lived on God. And every day, he would start over again. He always found new words to pray, to speak with the Lord.

Later, there would be an evening audience for his closest collaborators: on Mondays and Thursdays, the secretary of state; on Tuesdays, the undersecretary; on Wednesdays, the secretary of the Second Section of the Secretariat, whom the journalists call the "foreign minister"; on Fridays, the prefect (Cardinal Ratzinger, beginning in 1981) or the secretary of the Congregation for the Doctrine of the Faith; and on Saturdays, the prefect of the Congregation of Bishops.

Then it was time for dinner, which he also shared with guests, such as representatives of the Curia, the directors of the Press Office and L'Osservatore Romano, or collaborators working with the Pope on speeches or agendas. Sometimes the guests would be friends passing through Rome, such as Father Tadeusz Styczeń, his successor in the chair of ethics at Lublin, who would spend vacations with him.

John Paul II's house was always open. And he liked to be with other people, to listen to them, to take an interest in their problems, to discuss issues and events with them. He had cordial relations with Italian politicians, too. For example, the president of the Italian Republic, Sandro Pertini, was very close to the Pope. After the assassination attempt, he stayed at Gemelli until the operation was over. He would call the Pope a lot and would drop in to say good-bye before he went away on vacation. Another person was President Carlo Azeglio Ciampi and his first lady, Franca, who was always concerned about the Holy Father's health.

The Pope always wanted to be informed about everything. He read the press roundup and L'Osservatore Romano. And in the evening, he would also watch TV, on the set that was kept in the dining room, off to the left. He would watch the first part of the news, but also programs recorded on videocassette, like documentaries. But he wasn't averse to movies. He would say, "They get me thinking."

After dinner, he would deal with the documents sent over (always in an old threadbare bag) from the Secretariat of State. Then he would spend some time reading for pleasure. He would read works of literature or books that had piqued his interest. Then he would visit the chapel for the last prayer, the last conversation with the Lord. His final act every evening was to look out his bedroom window at Rome, which was by now all lit up, and give the city his blessing. And with that sign of the cross over "his" city, he would close the day and go to sleep.

14.

A Sign of Change

Right from the beginning, from the moment of his election, Karol Wojtyla's papacy was marked by change. For the first time in 455 years, a non-Italian—the first Pole; indeed, the first representative of Slavic Catholicism—had been elected Pope. Of course, the tradition John Paul II's pontificate changed was by now partly obsolete, if not actually indefensible.

At the origin of the shift was the Second Vatican Council. It presented to the world a thoroughly renewed image of the Church. The Church no longer merely claimed to be universal (while actually remaining very Eurocentric and Western), but was now really acting universally in history.

And yet, it was surely no small matter for the Church to break with a custom that had endured for almost half a millennium.

There were some people who thought it might stir up resentment and prejudice that could create an unfavorable attitude toward the new Pope. Even Cardinal Wyszynski was worried. I know that he said to an Italian journalist, "Help Wojtyla become popular." And the journalist replied, "But Your Eminence, John

Paul II has already won everybody over! Just look at that speech he made right after his election."

So the election of a non-Italian was the radical change, both on an institutional and a pastoral level. There was a second change closely connected with the first: the change embodied by the new Pope himself, by what formed him both as a priest and as a man, and by his experience as a Pole who had lived through two tragedies: first the war and the Nazi occupation and then communism.

That's an observation that the Holy Father himself frequently made, even in public speeches. His firsthand experience of the two totalitarianisms that rocked humanity in the twentieth century left a deep mark on his life and his mission, first as a bishop and then as the head of the universal Church. It was that experience that gave birth to his passionate defense of the dignity of the human person and his commitment to peace and justice in the world, priorities that would then characterize his entire pontificate.

All in all, then, it was quite a different papacy from the ones preceding it. This was partly due to its historical setting, which was a special time both for the Church and for the world. Another source of innovation and originality was the very personal way in which John Paul II interpreted his role as Peter. As Pope, he was more than the face of institutional leadership (although I don't mean to cast aspersions on the Popes who were). He was a charismatic prophet and missionary. And his anticonformism was so spontaneous and natural that it didn't really cause any shock in ecclesiastical circles.

You could say that he effected a quiet revolution, but a revolution it was.

Karol Wojtyla had an inborn independence, although he obviously asked for collaboration and knew how to consult. To begin with, he was an attentive listener. When people proposed their ideas to him, he would ponder them seriously. He informed himself, he read about everything, but make no mistake: He wasn't an imitator. Once he had gotten a sufficiently clear grasp of the basic framework of a given problem, he would typically begin with a concise summary of the issue. He would go on from there to develop his ideas with great freedom until he had worked out a definite approach.

This helps us understand better the sort of relations Pope John Paul II had with the Roman Curia. That is, it proves the falsity of many "legends" to the effect that he attached little importance to the central government of the Church. Or that it took the Roman Curia a while to accept fully this outsider Pope, who had very different notions about the world and history.

Every Pope leads the Church and the Roman Curia in the way that's most congenial to his personality, his sensibility, and his vision of the Catholic community. John Paul II was no exception. His very moral authority, activity, and initiatives already implied a whole program for magisterial teaching and mission, and the insitutions followed along with full conviction.

On the whole, I have to say that the Pope regarded the collaboration of the Roman Curia as both invaluable and indispensable. He accorded it a lot of freedom to draft documents and he always showed great respect for the people who worked on them.

But then he was the one who would make the final decision—with full autonomy.

For example, when the long and complicated process of updating the Code of Canon Law was approaching completion, they brought him a copy of their proposed final version. The authors thought their job was done, but the Pope called them back and told them that he had read the text three times and had found a certain number of points requiring revision. So over the next few days, he went through the entire draft with them paragraph by paragraph.

In fact, John Paul II invented a new way of exercising the papacy, which was especially evident in how he related with people and served them as a pastor. He also invented a new way of governing, whose main instrument was his travels, which gave the papal office an itinerant, authentically apostolic character.

Furthermore, we need to remember that as a young man Karol Wojtyla had acted on the stage, an experience that had taught him the art of communication. His philosophical studies and his background in personalism no doubt reinforced his proclivity for personal relations. Finally, he had a great concern for young people and for couples, and he proposed a whole new kind of catechesis, which was open to people's doubts and existential questionings.

Well, without his ever fully realizing it, all of this had prepared him to be a communicator Pope. But he communicated with a natural and unaffected ease. He was always natural. Take his gestures, or his improvisational way of saying what was on his mind, or especially his talent for giving each of his listeners, no matter how far away they were, the impression that he was talking to or thinking only of them.

✦ ✦ ✦

That reminds me of one of the Wednesday general audiences. A priest was there with a group of young women. They were all former prostitutes who had decided to turn over a totally new leaf. When their turn came, they all burst into tears. One by one, they came toward the Pope with eyes full of tears, and shame, and maybe even a bit of embarrassment. The Pope's reaction? He embraced them and gave them his blessing.

That was Karol Wojtyla: He welcomed everyone with respect and love. Every woman, every man, was equally important. And not because of their social status, or their job, or because they had a famous name.

For him, it didn't matter whom he was talking to. Whether they were the great of this world, like the heads of state, or whether he was dealing with humble, modest people, they were always treated as persons possessing equal dignity. They were always, all of them, children of God.

The journalists started calling him the "Great Communicator." That tag was certainly a bit triumphalistic, but it was based on something true. For it nicely captured the Pope's identity as a missionary who went forth to carry the Gospel to every continent. Obviously, though, he preached the Gospel in the context of today's world, applying it to the concrete situations of our time. And this explains why he exposed himself to the world of the media, which he made abundant use of, but was never imprisoned by.

He had no strategy. Wojtyla was an authentic man to the core. He was a shepherd and his job was to evangelize. But doesn't evangelization mean "proclaiming the Good News"? And when we translate that into today's language, doesn't it mean "communication"?

From the beginning of his pontificate, then, John Paul II did nothing but fulfill the same mission as the Apostles, the mission, that is, of proclaiming, of communicating, the message of the Gospel everywhere. And not once did he ever water down the message out of fear that the media might inflate the "unpopularity" of what he was saying.

Marshall McLuhan used to argue that "the medium is the message." The Pope, however, turned the terms of the problem upside down. He always used the media as just that: a means, an instrument, and never as an end. He accepted the laws and rules of the media, and he ran the corresponding risks, but he was never subject to them, and he never let himself be exploited into a media spectacle.

Once, he did seem to act on diametrically opposite principles. When he came back from Gemelli the second time in the final days of his life, there was a TV camera behind him in the car, transmitting live images of his whole ride home to the Vatican. But this was due to an imprudent decision taken by someone else. The Pope merely put up with it, and in retrospect he was very unhappy about what had happened. But it was really an exception due to the dramatic circumstances of the moment.

Yes. I see quite different images and memories in my mind's eye.

I think back to Fatima, when the Holy Father spent a long time praying before the statue of the Virgin. Or of the time in the Wawel Cathedral, when he remained at least thirty minutes praying before the tomb of Saint Stanislas.

And both times, the cameramen had to bend themselves to the Pope's silence. The whole time—an incredibly, in fact unbearably, long time for television—they were obliged to keep filming the same motionless, soundless scene. There was nothing for them to film—except that man, dressed in white, kneeling, completely absorbed in prayer.

Of course, the Holy Father wasn't forcing his silence on the television. He only did what he felt like he had to do spiritually. He prayed.

15.

Peter the Traveler

If he wasn't the most well traveled man in history, he was at least the most well traveled Pope of all times. No Pontiff had ever visited more countries. He was seen in person by a half a billion people, maybe more. If you work it all out, his travels add up to about thirty or so circumnavigations of the globe, which is more than three times the distance from the Earth to the Moon. And yet, it all started by chance.

To be sure, the new Pope was young, just fifty-eight when he was elected. Plus, he was willing to travel, partly because of the experience he had garnered during his tenure in Kraków. Furthermore, the very situation in which Catholicism found itself demanded a different way of exercising the papacy. For, while the Pope is the successor of Peter, he is also, as Wojtyla himself reminded us, the heir of that great traveler named Paul. There was that old invitation to visit Mexico. . . .

The Holy Father accepted immediately. He said, "We can't wait for the faithful to show up in Saint Peter's Square; we have to go to them." Plus, how many people have the chance to go to Rome to meet the Pope? So he thought that it was the Pope's—and the Church's—special duty to seek man in the footsteps of Christ, who walked the Earth teaching. And that's why John Paul II's entire apostolic activity was to be an itinerant teacher.

After Mexico came Poland. That was followed by several pearls on the string of new invitations: Ireland, the United States and the UN, Turkey. And these first journeys already clearly embodied the big priorities of this missionary Pope: the confrontation with both the Communist world and liberal society, ecumenical and interreligious dialogue, and so forth.

I have to say that I—much more than the Holy Father—was rather shocked by the reception at the Ankara airport. It was a pro forma gesture, with very few words wasted. And the streets of the city were almost empty. It was nothing compared with the enthusiasm of the previous trips. But then, Turkey is a constitutionally secular country, which at the same time happens to be almost 100 percent Muslim. In spite of everything, though, it ended up being an important trip. The Pope was able to meet with the Orthodox patriarch of Constantinople and to initiate a dialogue with Islam.

Little by little, a picture emerged, not merely of the strategy but also of the deep, innovative meaning behind John Paul II's pilgrimages to what he called the "living sanctuary of the people of God." And so the trips became more and more systematic and institutional. Indeed, they ended up becoming an integral part of the Pope's ministry and even of his governance of the Church.

◆   ◆   ◆

These trips gave Catholicism greater universality and a new missionary impetus. They consolidated the links between the Holy See and the local churches, which, in turn, found new strength and unity because of the trips. After a papal pilgrimage, there was often an increase both in vocations (in Eastern Europe and Africa, for example) and in conversions (as in South Korea, even though it is a predominantly Buddhist and Confucianist country). Sometimes, too, the spiritual climate of the event ended up spreading throughout the entire country and in some way transforming it.

Pope John Paul II celebrated Mass in the city squares, stadiums, and airports. He attracted increasingly impressive crowds of young people. Away from home, he was always at ease when appearing in public. In fact, he seemed to be more truly himself, more free of constraints, outside of Italy than in the Vatican palaces. "Every day," he once confided, "I traverse a spiritual geography. My spirituality is somewhat geographical."

John Paul II always kept within reach a big atlas, where he marked the dioceses from every country in the world. And he knew by heart the names of all the ordinaries. So when he received the bishops in audience, they didn't even have to remind him where they came from.

But there were criticisms, as well: The critics objected that there were too many trips, that they were too politicized, and that they were too expensive.

The criticisms were mean-spirited and agenda-driven. The point is that the Pope was becoming a disturber of the peace, because his mere presence was enough to call into question ideologies of whatever stripe. He, at any rate, tried to make people understand. He said he was being led by Providence, which sometimes pushed him to do things *per excessus* (to excess). Once, though, I did see him get really angry.

He was coming back from Thailand, where he had visited one of ten huge camps built to shelter refugees from Southeast Asia. During his visit, he had vigorously appealed to the international community to do something about this dire situation. On the plane, a journalist said to him, "You raised the political issue of the refugees." He replied with something like ire in his voice: "It's a human issue—human! It's not about politics. Reducing this to politics is all wrong. The basic human issue is morality."

So began the period of the major pilgrimages: Africa, Asia, and Latin America. John Paul II visited countries marred by poverty and injustice, countries still subjected to base exploitation by the First World. He visited places like the Senegalese island of Gorée, the site of the "unknown holocaust" perpetrated against millions of black Africans who left there in chains for the Americas.

In the evening, after his visit to the slave island, the Holy Father couldn't stop talking about it. He was horrified and anguished, especially on account of the children victimized by the obscenity of the slave trade. And he couldn't reconcile himself to the fact that the culprits of such a horrible crime were men who professed to be Christians.

How many memories, though!

Once, in Chad, he was in a motorcade wending its way down a road on the edge of the Sahel. They happened to pass a little village that consisted of no more than a few rude huts. The Holy Father asked them to stop. He then proceeded to enter one of the hovels and talk with the people there. He wanted to see; he wanted to understand. And what he saw and understood may be the reason he later spoke so emphatically of the world community's duty not to forget Africa.

In Brazil, they took the Pope to a *favela* (shantytown). The poverty was frightening. I remember his eyes. He kept looking around, almost in despair because he didn't know what he could do to relieve the suffering of the people in that particular place and at that particular moment. And then he surprised everyone by taking off his papal ring and giving it to the inhabitants.

Another time on the same trip—it was in Teresina, I think— he was celebrating Mass or a liturgy of the Word. They had just started reciting the Our Father when the Pope saw a sign that said "Holy Father, the people are hungry." And then he continued: "Give daily bread today to this people suffering from hunger." After having encountered the dramatic situation on the ground during that first visit to Brazil, the Pope changed 50 percent of the text of his speech to the bishops that had been prepared in Rome.

In Popayán, Colombia, there was a meeting with the *indios*. Their chief began reading his entire, uncut greeting, not the version that had been censored beforehand. He had hard words for the landowners who ordered the killing of the Indians, including women and children. A priest jumped onto the stage and took the microphone away from him, but John Paul II told him to keep speaking. At that moment, I thought that one gesture like that was worth a hundred speeches.

✦   ✦   ✦

Two countries went to war in 1982: England and Argentina were fighting over possession of the Falkland Islands (or Malvinas).

The Holy Father happened to be visiting Great Britain. Although the trip had been planned for some time, the Argentine government protested. The result was that within less than twenty-four hours, a new trip was organized.

In just a week's time, the Pope got on an airplane and headed to Buenos Aires. Between the flight out (with a layover in Rio de Janeiro) and the flight back, he endured twenty-nine hours on the plane, whereas he spent only twenty-eight hours on Argentine soil—just enough time to speak words of peace that proved key for averting an escalation of the conflict.

The Pope also made visits to countries torn by civil war, such as Angola and East Timor, and to countries that had just emerged from civil war, such as Lebanon and Bosnia.

The Pope visited Sarajevo in April 1997. But he was already supposed to have gone three years earlier. At that time, the trip organizers informed him that the situation wasn't yet stable and that his safety would be at risk. His answer: "Risk is normal for the Pope. If missionaries, bishops, and nuncios take risks, why shouldn't the Pope take them, too?"

But just when everything was ready, they told him that General Rose, the supreme commander of NATO forces in Sarajevo, had very frankly said that while he could protect the Pope, he wasn't able to guarantee security for the people. At that point, the Holy Father decided not to go: "It's not right to place the life of a single person in jeopardy!"

◆   ◆   ◆

John Paul II never held back. He went to hostile countries, such as Nicaragua under the Sandinistas, or to countries still deprived of freedom by oppressive regimes, like many of the petty dictatorships in Africa, or Pinochet's Chile, or Fidel Castro's Cuba.

In Nicaragua, they organized a shameful protest against the Pope. Later, it came to light that they had even brought over experts from Poland to advise them about how to manipulate microphones and TV broadcasts.

The Holy Father almost single-handedly faced the mob and stood up to the provocateurs. There was an unforgettable scene with the Sandinistas waving their red-and-black flags on the one side, and the Pope on the other side, holding up his staff with the crucifix on top.

That said, he suffered a lot—really a lot—because of that. He suffered because of the profanation of the Eucharist, but also because the Sandinistas had prevented the faithful from reaching the place of the celebration. Those who did manage to get through were confined to an area far away from the altar and the Pope, where they couldn't hear his homily.

He only recovered when he got back to San José, Costa Rica, and was greeted by a huge crowd who came to express all their solidarity with, and love for, him.

The trip to Chile was a difficult one, too. There were some who were obviously trying to manipulate the visit, as well as people on the other side who wanted to take advantage of the Pope's presence to discredit the Pinochet regime internationally.

During the beatification of Saint Teresa de los Andes in Santiago's main park, the opposition raised a ruckus, and the police reacted with tear gas and shots in the air. The smoke reached all the way to the altar. The Pope wasn't personally alarmed, but for the rest of the Mass, he was worried about the people, afraid that something serious might happen to them.

The journalists gave that disgraceful episode a lot of coverage but said almost nothing about John Paul II's meeting with the youth in the national stadium. It was really exciting. He was shouting, *"El amor es más fuerte"*—"Love is stronger." And when he asked if they were ready to renounce the "idols" of the world, the young people all shouted back, *"Sí."* Maybe that yes was the beginning of a new chapter in Chile's history.

Here's something no one talked about at the time: After being forced to appear with Pinochet on the balcony of the presidential palace, the Holy Father suggested to him in a private meeting that the time had come to return power to the civil authorities. Then, a few hours later, he met with the leaders of all the political parties that were still outlawed at the time.

On the one hand, then, the trips were mainly spiritual events that set the stage for what in some countries was an extraordinary religious renewal. On the other hand, they gave John Paul II a forum to speak his mind freely to dictators on the Right and on the Left, and in that way to speak for all those people who weren't allowed to express themselves.

The trips thus gave the Pope a venue for developing a very vigorous campaign in defense of human rights, social justice, and peace. You might say that he supported the process of democratization in Latin America, the transition to political and cultural emancipation in at least some African and Asian coun-

tries, and the gradual decline of communism in Eastern Europe.

The fall of the Berlin Wall opened the doors of the former USSR to the Holy Father. The first country to open up was Czechoslovakia. It was gradually followed by the rest, from Albania to the Baltic republics, from Bulgaria, to Ukraine, to distant places like Armenia, Georgia, Kazakhstan, and Azerbaijan, where the Catholic community numbers just a few hundred people.

The papal visits were often requested by the heads of state themselves. This was the case in Byelorussia, although the authorities later dropped the invitation without explaining why. On the other hand, the president of Mongolia invited the Pope with the words "Hurry up and come! We need you!" The government had already granted freedom of worship to Muslims and Buddhists, but they obviously thought that the presence of a body like the Catholic Church would contribute to the moral and social progress of the nation.

It's a shame that the Pope wasn't able to make the pilgrimage to Mongolia. John Paul II was planning to stop in Russia for the official handover of the so-called Kazan icon of the Mother of God, at which point he would continue on to Mongolia. It's a real shame the trip didn't come off, because it would have been a good opportunity for him to meet with the patriarch of Moscow, Alexei II, something that had already failed to materialize twice before.

Nevertheless, the papal trips did promote rapprochement between the Church of Rome and other Christian churches. This was partly due to the humility with which the Pope often acknowledged the past "sins" of Catholics during his pilgrimages.

◆ ◆ ◆

I'd like to recall the Holy Father's visit to Greece. The invitation had come from the president, whereas the Holy Synod of the Orthodox Church went only so far as to say that it "wasn't opposed," though it made no secret of its displeasure. This attitude reflected centuries-old baggage: opposition, misunderstanding, and mutual accusation.

Well, all the Pope had to do was ask forgiveness for the "sack of Constantinople" by Latin Christians during the Fourth Crusade, and the atmosphere changed completely. On the face of Christodoulos, the Orthodox archbishop of Athens, I read not only great surprise but also great joy, to which he immediately added his sincere applause.

The next day, there was another very significant ecumenical moment. After the private interview in the nunciature, the Holy Father and Christodoulos were leaving the room side by side. John Paul II turned to his companion and the other Orthodox dignitaries and said, "Let's say the Our Father now; you say it in Greek, and we'll say it in Latin." And they recited the prayer on the spot. That common prayer, that first prayer together, was like the seal of reconciliation. And there has been a fraternal dialogue between the two churches ever since.

At the same time, the papal pilgrimages contributed to overcoming the obstacles and complications to a renewal of relations with Judaism and Islam, which had proved challenging in the past. The visit to the Rome synagogue—the first by any Pope—could be considered both the shortest (just a few kilometers from the Vatican) and the longest (twenty centuries of history) of the trips undertaken by the head of the Catholic Church. And the visit to the mosque in Damascus—also a papal first—was likewise the fruit of a courageous trip to a difficult country.

Of course, there were some countries, such as China and Vietnam, that refused to open their doors, and there were some painful refusals, such as Russia and Iraq. In spite of that, it must be acknowledged that John Paul II's journeys not only influenced the different stages of his pontificate but also forged a link, indeed, a spiritual bridge, between the First World and the Third World, the East and the West. The Pope shortened geographical and cultural distances and opened many political and ideological borders. Above all, though, he brought nations and peoples closer together. He helped them to live out the values of universal brotherhood and solidarity, and thus rediscover the common destiny that binds them together.

16.

Rome's Own Bishop

Wojtyla discovered Rome as a young, newly ordained priest. He had been sent there to finish his studies and he quickly got to know the city, to understand its spirit, and to love it. He breathed in a spirit of universality that would stick with him forever.

So when he was elevated to the papacy, he felt fully "Roman." Not a monarch, or a head of state, but the Bishop of Rome.

That was something very real for the Holy Father, something that he experienced very intensely and would often mention in his speeches. If he was the Pope, the head of the whole Catholic community, then it was because he had succeeded Peter as the bishop of the particular Church of Rome. It was this Roman commitment that invigorated his universal mission, not the other way around. And that's precisely why he wanted Rome to be a model diocese in its own right, and not just an appendage of the Vatican.

So for John Paul II, being Bishop of Rome wasn't just a matter of having another title, but involved—perhaps more than it ever had for any previous Pope—the actual exercise of the ministry, of the munus (duty), that went with it. And he wasted no time making that known. At his first meeting with the bishops' committee (Cardinal Ugo Poletti and the auxiliary bishops), he announced that he intended to visit "his" parishes. On December 3, 1978, just forty-eight days after his election, he visited San Francesco Saverio, in the Garbatella neighborhood not far from the EUR park.

It was the same parish where Karol Wojtyla used to say Mass every Sunday during his first period in Rome. At that time, a van used to drive around to all the ecclesiastical institutes (he was staying at the Belgian College in those days) to pick up non-Italian priests and seminarians who were studying in Rome. It would drop them off around 9:00 A.M. in the various parishes, where they would help out with pastoral work until the van picked them up again after noon. Well, Father Karol's parish happened to be the one you mentioned, San Francesco Saverio. That's where, struggling a bit with Italian, he would hear confessions.

The Pope returned to "his" parish on a cold, wintry afternoon, but all the people in the neighborhood were waiting there to greet him. There was such a large crowd that a lot of people were forced to stand outside the church.

Standing on the balcony of the parish hall, he spoke to the young people who were in the courtyard of the church. A young woman from Catholic Action greeted him very familiarly: "Welcome, Brother, in our midst." And he adapted himself to the setting, to the audience, to their enthusiasm. He spoke extemporaneously, and when it was over, they didn't want him to leave.

The Mass began and a lot of people were amazed by some-
thing new that he did. At a certain point, John Paul II invited all
the married couples to join hands and—there, before the Bishop
of Rome—to renew the vows they had exchanged on their wed-
ding day. This was a practice he had initiated in Kraków when-
ever he would visit a parish.

For a lot of people—perhaps including some people in the Vatican—it must have seemed obvious that the visit to Garbatella
was, shall we say, a farewell to his old life and his long experience as a pastor in Poland, since now that he was Pope, he would
have to dedicate himself to the universal Church. Or, at most,
people thought that even if the visit was a meaningful gesture, it
was one that he wouldn't be repeating very often.

Instead, it turned out to be the beginning of a real pilgrimage
in the true sense of the word, the beginning of an extended pastoral visit to the diocese of Rome. And the parishes gave the Holy
Father a chance to improve his acquaintance with the city. They
were his road into the heart of Rome.

John Paul II traveled around the world, but when he got back
from his exhausting tours, he would set out again to visit a new
parish—at least fifteen every year. His commitment to the parish
visitations was unwavering and systematic. He never broke the
continuity except for exceptional reasons (the trips) or serious
problems (the assassination attempt, health issues, accidents).
And whenever he had stopped, he would start again. And he
continued even after age and illness had weakened his body.

On the Wednesday before every visit, he would have a lunchtime
meeting with the parish priest, his assistant priests, the cardinal

Lewes Public Library
111 Adams Ave.
Lewes, DE 19958
302-645-2733
www.leweslibrary.org
M-TH: 10-8, F: 10-5, SAT: 10-2

User name: MCGANN, WILLIAM

Date due: 9/8/2011, 23:59
Title: A life with Karol : my
forty-year friendship with
Item ID: 33806001614990
Date charged: 8/18/2011, 14:
37

Thank you for supporting
Delaware libraries
Delaware Library Catalog
http://www.lib.de.us

vicar (first it was Ugo Poletti, then Camillo Ruini), and the auxiliary bishop of the area. They prepared a report for him on the
parish, its pastoral issues, the difficulties it faced, and, of course,
the people who attended it. And the Holy Father wouldn't just
listen; he would ask questions, inform himself, in order to get a
precise, detailed picture of that portion of the people of God.

Then, on the Sunday of the visit, the Pope went to get personally
acquainted with the parish and its people, especially its families.
He chatted with the teenagers and the kids. One time, a young
man reminded him a bit mischievously of a soccer score: "Italy
two, Poland zero, Your Holiness." Another one gave him his
phone number—"in case you want to call me." They wanted to
know everything about him: why he had decided to become a
priest; if he was strict; whether he was happy with the job. And
he answered their questions, explained things, told stories.

Another big interest of his was the university students. They
were one of his constant concerns. He always used to say that
how the rising generations were shaped would determine what a
society or nation would look like in the future. This is why, when
he was just starting, he complained that there was no specific
ministry for college kids. This dearth eventually led him to or-
ganize his annual meetings with university students.

The Pope would end up visiting almost all the parishes of
Rome—more than three hundred in toto. But that was not all.
There were the meetings with the clergy, the Corpus Christi pro-
cession, the prayer to Mary Immaculate in the Piazza di Spagna,
the end-of-the-year Te Deum, and the traditional meetings with
the authorities.

Day after day, then, Pope John Paul II succeeded in penetrating to the heart of Rome—not just the Rome of religion and spirituality but the Rome of society, culture, and politics, as well. He spoke out against the city's progressive de-Christianization and denounced its urban and human blight. Once, particularly struck by what he had seen on the outskirts of the city, he exclaimed, "There are pockets of the Third World here!"

On his way to a visit in the parish of San Paulo della Croce one Sunday, he discovered what the Romans call the "serpent's tail," a half-mile-long housing complex, where thousands of people live crowded together, without—at least back then—any social services. There was crime and drug trafficking everywhere. It was so bad that even the police stayed away.

The Holy Father was deeply troubled. He wondered how people could live this way. But faced with such a happy and cheerful crowd, he took refuge in irony. As he was taking his leave, he said, "You inhabitants of this"—he stopped to find the right word—"this amazing palace."

By this time, even Rome was a secularized city. The time had come to start thinking about how to repair the Christian fabric of society. Such an undertaking, however, mainly required new approaches, directions, and methods. The Pope convoked a synod to implement Vatican II in the different areas of pastoral concern. He promoted the so-called City Mission to rouse believers out of their anonymity, their comfortable "hiding places" in the parishes, and to give the Church new missionary dynamism.

And the Pope's spiritual and religious commitment to the city kept pace with his interest in its civil affairs.

◆ ◆ ◆

One Sunday, he was scheduled to visit a parish in the north, in the heart of the industrial district, the so-called Tiburtina Valley. It just so happened that there had been a new proposal that very week to transfer some businesses, especially some of the smaller ones, to other areas of the city. So thousands of families who lived and worked there were now possibly facing serious difficulties. And so the Holy Father met with owners and workers who were fighting side by side for what had become a common cause. The Pope listened to them and backed them publicly as far as he could.

The visit to the Campidoglio in mid-January 1998 was the final confirmation of Pope John Paul II's special concern for Rome and of the years of effort he had lavished to reawaken the city's awareness of the role it could continue to play in the international community. A role, by the way, that was fulfilled on the spiritual level by the Great Jubilee in the year 2000.

It took a Pope from Poland to remind us that Roma spelled backward is amor (love).

17.

Earthquake in the Empire

Poland couldn't believe its own eyes when it saw Karol Wojtyla driving through the streets of Warsaw in an open yellow-and-white car. Everywhere, he was greeted by a rain of petals descending from the housetops. The people were half-traumatized by emotion. All anyone could do was cry.

As the plane was beginning to land, John Paul II watched through the window as his country drew closer and closer. He was tense with emotion. And he spoke so softly that I was having trouble understanding him. He called that trip a "duty": "It was my duty to visit Poland! It was my duty to support the Polish people!"

He was the first Pope ever to set foot in a Communist country. And he was doing it in June 1979—at a time when Europe's heart was still cut in two by the Iron Curtain. Indeed, the whole world was cut in two ideologically. The international order, governed by the conflict between two superpowers, the United States and the Soviet Union, was based de facto on the balance

*of terrror, on the mutual fear of the possible outbreak of nu-
clear war.*

*This explains why the Kremlin had done all it could to prevent
John Paul II from returning to Poland. For days, Brezhnev kept
repeating the same mantra: "That man will bring nothing but
trouble!" And when the Communist leaders in Warsaw tried to
explain to the Soviet leader how difficult it was to say no to a
Polish Pope, he came up with an unbelievable suggestion: "The
Pope's a sensible fellow. Tell him to make a public statement to
the effect that he is indisposed and has to cancel the trip."*

Moscow was absolutely opposed to this trip. Then there was the
Polish regime, and that gave rise to another problem. You have to
remember that Saint Stanislas was killed by a tyrannous king
for having defended the people, but in the Communist version
of history, he was an inconvenient figure, someone who had
gone against the state. So the regime was terrified at the thought
that the papal visit might coincide with the ninth centenary
of the saint's martyrdom. But once the date of the trip was
changed, moved as far as possible from the ominous day, May 8,
it was a lot easier to prevail on the Warsaw government to give
its okay.

*The Pope celebrated the first Mass in Victory Square, where the
regime used to hold its most important public celebrations. And
that service, which was attended by a flood of people, was like
an image of the explosive event that Cardinal König said was
nothing less than a political earthquake. An apparently inde-
structible system, which had enforced its atheistic creed unop-
posed during more than thirty years of absolute rule, was
suddenly forced to be the mute and powerless witness of the*

symbolic collapse of its ideology, its power, and, one might even say, its spell.

In any case, the regime realized what was happening and tried to do some damage control—in its usual way, of course. All you had to do was watch TV to notice that. The frames were always narrow, because that way they could hide the enormous level of popular participation. And then, as we found out later, they had ordered that the TV cameras never show young people or children, but always focus on priests, sisters, handicapped people, and little old ladies.

June 2 was the Vigil of Pentecost, the birthday of the Church. So it was a day that also recalled the Baptism of Poland, the birth of Christianity in the nation. This is why the Pope said that "the exclusion of Christ from man's history is a crime against man. Without Him, the history of Poland makes no sense." At that point, the crowd burst into an amazing round of applause, which lasted for more than ten minutes. It sounded like the rumble of an earthquake. And the rumble grew louder and louder and took on an increasingly polemical edge. There's no question that its echo could be heard a long way off.

I don't think I'm exaggerating when I say that the atmosphere was almost supernatural. Plus, there was an incredibly deep and intense symbiosis between the Pope and the Polish people at that moment. Finally, when John Paul II practically shouted the prayer to the Holy Spirit, he was sincerely praying, but at that historical moment the invocation also had an obvious relevance to a Poland still living under oppression: "Send down Your Spirit!

Send down Your Spirit! And renew the face of the Earth. Of this Earth!"

After Warsaw, the Pope headed for Gniezno, the birthplace of Christian Poland. The "Slavic Pope"—as he called himself there for the first time—wanted to help the peoples of the neighboring countries reclaim their voice and reenter the circle of the international community. So he gave the "Church of silence" a chance to speak, a chance to emerge from the catacombs where it had been forced into hiding. Above all, though, the Pope rehabilitated the idea that Europe is a spiritual unity based on shared Christian roots. And that was an indirect denunciation of the "logic" that Stalin had forced on the Allies at Yalta in order to divide the continent in two.

At Gniezno, the Holy Father also spoke of the rights of man and of nations. He spoke of moral solidarity. The Solidarity Union didn't exist at the time, so what he meant was solidarity among human beings. Those words were a great support not only for Poles but also for all the neighboring peoples.

A proof of what I'm saying is that the Pope's overture toward all the Eastern-bloc countries immediately caused the hearts of the Communist party bosses to skip a few beats. They were extremely worried. And that was when the first warnings started to come: "The Pope can deal with these matters if he wants to— better if he doesn't do it here, though, but outside Poland."

Cardinal Wyszynski had his worries, too, although they obviously came from a different source. He had to think about how, given this new situation, he was supposed to manage relations with the regime after the Pope's departure.

◆ ◆ ◆

It was already obvious that John Paul II had changed the Church's method of dealing with the Communist world. The older approach had used diplomacy to negotiate freedoms for the Church. John Paul II added a new strategy, one focusing on religion, civil engagement, and culture. The Vatican Ostpolitik thus got updated in light of an overarching commitment to respect for human rights. In short, the Pope gave pride of place to dialogue with peoples (the heirs of a given cultural patrimony) and nations (the guarantors of national identity), rather than with states and governments.

The authorities in Warsaw were not acting like Poles; that much is certain. Their determination to give the papal visit the lowest-possible profile, their manipulation of the television coverage, their effort to throw up a bunch of ridiculous obstacles in the way of the people, especially by making it hard for the buses to shuttle the pilgrims around—all of that, as I was just saying, had nothing to do with Poland or its traditions of hospitality, even less so given that they were dealing with a Polish Pope on top of everything else. I've no doubt that the authorities were bowing to pressures coming from Moscow as well as from Prague. They were terrified of how Big Brother might react.

What is more, the Communist bosses were doubly terrified, because they were beginning to realize that the situation was slipping out of their control. The Pope was using words that they had long since expunged from the dictionary. And, in his address to the bishops gathered at Czestochowa, he said in no uncertain terms that respect for human rights was the prior condition sine qua non for the normalization of relations between Church and state; that Poles needed to start thinking of themselves and their country in a "European context"; and that Christianity needed to renew its engagement on behalf of Europe's spiritual unity. "Economic and political considerations aren't sufficient," he said.

By saying that, the Pope made it clear to everyone that he had never accepted Yalta and its division of Europe into two blocs, and that Yalta was a great injustice—perpetrated with the complicity of the Western powers to boot.

That speech, coming on the heels of his remarks in Gniezno, caused additional anxiety in the politburo. The number of protests and criticisms increased, as well. But, as far as I know, the Party representatives confined themselves to referring them to Bishop Bronislaw Dabrowski, the secretary of the Polish Bishops' Conference, who was the liaison with the Party.

Some journalist friends of mine did tell me, though, that at that point their "controllers" began ratcheting up the pressure—which was already suffocating—to get them to persuade representatives of the foreign press to come around to the regime's point of view.

But then there was the visit to Auschwitz.

The stage with the altar was set up in the nearby camp of Birkenau (Brzezinka), on the platform where they used to unload the sealed boxcars carrying deported Jews from all over Europe. "I could not fail to come here as Pope," John Paul II said. "I come to kneel at this Golgotha of the contemporary world."

And as he spoke of the plaques commemorating the victims of Hitler's insanity, he added an unexpected remark. He also mentioned the Russian plaque as a way of highlighting the suf-

ferings of the Russians in the struggle for the "freedom of peoples" during World War II.

It was right to acknowledge the Russians. And then, why not do something to defuse the tension in the air when the opportunity presented itself?

The final stop on the Pope's trip was his beloved Kraków. That was when the big party broke out. On the last day of his visit, there were almost two million people gathered in the gigantic esplanade of Blonie Park. To conclude the jubilee of Saint Stanislas, the Pope celebrated the Mass of the Most Holy Trinity. Both things—the jubilee and the Mass of the Trinity—called attention to one of the fundamental stages of Christian existence, the stage of mature responsibility that comes with the sacrament of Confirmation.

Right. Between the Baptism of Warsaw and the Confirmation of Kraków you had a summary of the deep meaning of the entire trip. The visit was most importantly about strengthening Poland's Christian faith, in which the nation had built its history, created its culture, and forged its inheritance. So the Pope was calling Poles back to their origins, to the meaning of the Polish legacy down through the centuries. At the same time, he was inviting them to keep faith with this heritage, to strengthen it, and to translate it into an unfailing defense of the dignity of the human person.

It was unforgettable! We felt as if something were happening, as if it were happening right above us. What was going on, I think, is that the people, with the Pope at their side, were beginning to feel free, interiorly free, and to stop being afraid. And

I don't mean just the people of Poland, but the people of other countries, too, especially among our neighbors in Eastern Europe. Even in the Third World, they were realizing that the Pope's very presence created an atmosphere of freedom.

And that's exactly what made John Paul II's pontificate powerful and new: He freed people from fear!

Meanwhile, the Communist regime was busily dismantling piece by piece the yellow-and-white car in which the Pope had ridden during his visit. I suppose they thought they were going to wipe out every reminder that the Pope had been present on Polish soil.

18.

A Revolution of
the People

*Before boarding the plane back to Rome at the Kraków airport,
the Pope said a last farewell to Henryk Jablonski, the president of
the Polish Council of State, planting a Slavic kiss on Jablonski's
very embarrassed cheeks. A few minutes earlier, the Pope had
added an important line to his farewell speech: "This unprecedented event is without a doubt an act of courage on both sides."*

The Pope added those words because he wanted to express his
satisfaction that the visit had gone so well. And above all, he
wanted to thank the authorities for the courage they had shown,
which explains his departure from protocol with Jablonski. He
also meant, I think, the courage they had shown in allowing the
visit against the wishes of Moscow.

*"Nevertheless," the Pope continued, "an act of courage like this
is necessary in our day. We need to have the courage to strike out
in a hitherto untrodden direction."* In a certain sense, he was en-
couraging the leaders in Warsaw—and not just them—to keep

*in mind the positive things that had happened during the trip.
"Our times demand that we stop locking ourselves away behind
the rigid borders of systems, but that we seek everything necessary for the common good."*

*Unfortunately, in the months that followed, both Warsaw and
Moscow confirmed their by now congenital incapacity to emerge
from the state of rigid immobility into which the Communist
world had sunk.*

Karol Wojtyla's Polish experience had given him a real familiarity
with Marxist doctrine and its concrete applications. So he didn't
believe that the Communist system was capable of evolution. He
also didn't believe that there could be such a thing as communism "with a human face," because Marxism takes away man's
freedom, and so limits his ability to act and to develop.

On top of that, Marxist ideology claimed that religion is the
"opium of the people." So it engaged in propaganda on behalf of
atheism and didn't recognize the freedom of conscience or of religious bodies. So it was hard to reconcile the position of the
Church with Marxism and communism.

*The Pope's visit had engendered a new atmosphere in Poland.
There were signs of a widespread commitment to moral and social recovery. The dissenters grew bolder. The workers made in-
sistent pleas for recognition of their right to strike. The regime,
though, was unable to respond properly, or even with a minimum
of openness, to all of this. It fell back on the same old methods:
violence, intimidation, arrests, condemnations. It would soon
pay a steep price for that.*

*Something happened that had never happened before in the
Communist bloc.*

In the name of solidarity, the working class revolted against a deceitful ideology that for too long had falsely claimed to defend the interests of the workers and promised to establish the dictatorship of the proletariat. Really, though, it was the whole of Polish society that undermined the legitimacy of the system, by which it no longer felt represented morally, much less politically. By the same token, it was the whole of Polish society that demanded political structures for monitoring the administration of public affairs and the activities of the government.

July 1, 1980 . . .

It was immediately apparent that something was going to happen. No one knew exactly what it would be, but everyone knew that there was going to be a change. People remembered the first workers' protest, which took place in Poznań in 1956. With all of its defects, the 1956 protest did mark the beginning of a lot of new developments. The political climate changed, and Stalinism was left behind once and for all. Cardinal Wyszynski was released and the Church gained a little room for its mission. And, most important, the 1956 protest wasn't like the October uprising in Hungary, which ended with repression from outside the country.

On July 1, 1980, a few departments of the Ursus works near Warsaw suspended operations in the wake of a new increase in prices. The strike spread from there like an oil slick. This was in part because the authorities got frightened and lost their heads. They started making random economic concessions. They operated piecemeal, with no fixed plan: First they would give in to one factory, then another, then another. But this only succeeded in stoking the fires of protest. Finally, the wave of unrest reached the shores of the Baltic, where it sank down roots and became a permanent movement.

In the Lenin Shipyards in Gdańsk, a strike was called to protest the politically motivated firing of Anna Walentynowicz, a crane operator with twenty years' seniority, who also happened to be an activist in the workers' movement. The organizer of the strike was Lech Walesa, an electrician, who was one of the most visible members of the underground union. Images of the Black Madonna and pictures of the Polish Pope appeared on the gates of the shipyard. But the pictures that generated the most attention, and which were aired on TV around the world, were the ones showing the workers kneeling on the pavement to receive absolution so they could go to Mass and take Communion.

As soon as he saw that, the Holy Father exclaimed, "Maybe the moment has come! Well, well, this is incredible; it's never happened before! The workers are fighting for a just cause, to protest infringements of their right to work. And they're doing it peacefully. They're praying! They're proclaiming their faith in God and Our Lady! Their confidence in the Pope!"

Of course, those images were bound to make a big impression in countries that were either de-Christianized or whose working class had turned its back on the Church. But in Poland, despite years of communism and atheism, the workers hadn't abandoned God. On the contrary, the great majority of them were practicing believers who would rally to the Church in times of need, as they did in Nowa Huta.

Meanwhile, the workers put forward their demands, and a government delegation finally showed up for negotiations. However, neither of the two sides would give an inch. It looked as if things were going to take a turn for the worse. At that point, the authorities in Warsaw received the order from Moscow: "Sign! Sign! But put a stop to this agitation!" The leaders in the Kremlin, in Prague, and in the other Communist capitals were afraid that the Polish "plague" might spread and infect the other regions of an empire that already had enough problems on its hands.

Agreements were signed on August 30 in Szczecin and on August 31 in Gdańsk. The protocol included the acknowledgment of "autonomous, independent unions" and the guarantee of the right to strike. Solidarity, the first free union in Eastern Europe, was born. This occurred after sixty days of peaceful struggle that was respectful both of the geopolitical situation and of the constitution, but was also unrelenting in its call for the priority of the common good.

I remember that the Holy Father heaved a sigh of relief. He was extremely satisfied, not only because of the happy ending to the affair but also because there had been no need for violence or bloody battles to achieve it. And he was truly full of admiration at how the workers, finally conscious of their strength and the full legitimacy of their demands, had fought for freedom: for the freedom of the unions, of course, but also for freedom of religion; for salary increases, to be sure, but also for permission to broadcast Sunday Mass. In other words, it was a struggle in defense of man and his rights—and not just his material and economic ones but also his spiritual ones.

And if this was how the liberation movement was beginning, then it was very likely that the road would finally lead to the end of communism in Poland.

* ◆ ◆

In a word, then, Solidarity represented a return to the original inspiration behind the workers' movement: the idea that work is
subordinate to human growth and that workers' solidarity tran-
scends every sort of ideological or political opposition. These
same motifs reappeared later in the encyclical Laborem Ex-
ercens. Which goes to show that the Polish experience expressed
values that were regaining currency among workers everywhere,
values whose influence very probably extended far beyond the
boundaries of Poland.

This, of course, was exactly why the Communist regime tried
to destroy Solidarity.

As early as the fall of 1980, there were daily signals of mounting alarm in the Soviet-bloc countries about the events transpir-
ing in Poland. By now, all the Communist leaders were in
agreement that Solidarity was a dangerous bomb waiting to explode. Solidarity was dangerous not just because it might catch
on in other countries but also because its ideas amounted to an
attack on the very heart of Marxism.

The Holy See was receiving information to this effect from
various sources. The sources were mainly Church-related, but
information also came from Western, mostly American, secret
service agencies. This doesn't mean, though, that there was any
sort of "Holy Alliance" between the Vatican and the United
States.

There were direct contacts with the U.S. government. There
were telephone conversations, especially with Zbigniew Brzezinski, who at the time was the National Security Advisor. The
Americans would relay information that they had gathered con-

cerning possible threats to Poland posed by the Red Army or Soviet contingency plans for an invasion should tension escalate between government authorities and Solidarity.

There was nothing more to it than that. I repeat: It was just information, which, I think I can add, didn't contribute much to what the Apostolic See already knew from other sources.

At that point, though, John Paul II decided not to wait any longer. He took the initiative and made a bold step, whose very lack of precedence reflected the magnitude of the threat looming over Poland's future. On December 16, he wrote to Leonid Brezhnev, the president of the Soviet Union, in order to convey to him the full extent of "the concern felt by Europe and the world over the tension created by the events that have occurred inside of Poland in the last few months."

The tone of the letter was formal and diplomatic, but its substance was tough and unequivocal. The letter referred to the Nazi "aggression" of September 1939, an implicit parallel with the current situation that clearly conveyed the Pope's sharp disapproval of a possible Soviet invasion. There was a second reference to Polish history: the sacrifice of so many Poles during World War II. The letter then went on to recall the final Helsinki Accord. In other words, what happened in Poland was its own internal business and foreign interference was therefore totally inappropriate. "I trust," John Paul II wrote to Brezhnev, "that you wish to do everything in your power to defuse the present tension."

The Holy Father wrote Brezhnev because at the time he really feared an invasion of Poland. And he also wrote to defend the rights of the Polish nation, especially its right to decide its own destiny and its own internal affairs.

But there was nary a response to the Pope's letter. Not even indirectly through back channels. Nothing. The Kremlin, at that point, was a wall. An impenetrable wall.

Brezhnev never replied, probably becasuse he didn't want to tip his hand. Moscow had already decided. Solidarity couldn't be allowed to live. Too dangerous for the Soviet Empire!

19.

Two Pistol Shots

You want to know about that day? . . .

Every time I think about that day, the same thing always happens to me. It never fails. I relive the whole thing, moment by moment. It's as if I still can't quite bring myself to believe that anyone would go so far. That anyone would actually try to kill a Pope—*that* Pope, John Paul II—and to do it in the very heart of the Christian world.

That day, the jeep was making a second turn around Saint Peter's Square, in the direction of the right colonnade, which is the one that leads to the Bronze Gate. The Holy Father leaned out of the car to pick up a little blond girl her mom and dad were holding out to him. Her name was Sara. She wasn't even two years old, and she was clutching a piece of string tied to a colored balloon. He took her in his arms, lifted her into the air as if he wanted the whole world to see her, kissed her, and handed her back to her parents with a big smile.

I was charmed as I watched Sara's parents reach out to take back their little bundle of pink cotton. The exact time was 5:19, as we would later discover once the day's events had been reconstructed. In the summer, the Wednesday audiences were held in the afternoons in the open air. And that explains why we were circling the square in a jeep that day, May 13, 1981.

Then I heard the first shot. As it rang out, I noticed hundreds of pigeons suddenly lift off the ground and fly away in terror.

The second shot immediately followed. It was still echoing in my ears when the Holy Father went limp on one side and then collapsed into my arms.

Instinctively, I glanced in the direction where the shots had come from, although I would see it all again in the photographs and on television. In the midst of the tumult, a young man with dark features was trying to break loose from the crowd. Only later would I find out that it was the Pope's Turkish would-be assassin, Mehmet Ali Agca.

As I think back on it now, maybe I turned my eyes toward the commotion because I didn't want to see or accept the terrible thing that had just happened, even though I couldn't help feeling it in my arms.

I tried to help the Pope to his feet, but it was as if he had let himself go—gently. He was grimacing because of the pain, yet he was serene. I asked him, "Where?" He replied, "The stomach." "Does it hurt?" "Yes." The first bullet, we would learn, had pierced his abdomen, perforated the colon, torn through the small intestine at several points, and then come out the other side before finally lodging in the jeep. The second bullet had grazed his right elbow and broken his left index finger before going on to wound two American women.

Someone shouted the order to get an ambulance. But the ambulance was on the other side of the square. The jeep flew through the Arch of the Bells, made its way along via delle Fondamenta, circled round the back of the apse of the basilica, and then hurtled down the so-called Grottone, the courtyard of the Belvedere, before finally reaching the FAS, the Vatican health services. Renato Buzzonetti, the Holy Father's personal physician, had been summoned to meet us there.

They took the Pope from my arms and stretched him out on the floor of the lobby. It was only then that we realized how much blood he was losing from the first bullet wound. Buzzonetti bent his legs and asked him if he could move them. He could. Immediately after that, Buzzonetti shouted the order to rush the Pope to Gemelli. That wasn't a spur-of-the-moment decision, though, but a long-standing policy in case the Holy Father had to be hospitalized.

Meanwhile, the ambulance had pulled up. Once the Holy Father was inside, it took off at high speed, on a desperate race against time up via delle Medaglie d'Oro. The siren wasn't working and the traffic was a mess.

The Pope was fading, but he was still conscious. He was groaning quietly, and his voice kept getting weaker. He was praying, too. I heard him saying, "Jesus, Mother Mary."

As soon as we got to Gemelli, though, he lost consciousness. And at exactly that moment, it finally dawned on me that his life was in danger. Even the doctors who performed the surgery confessed to me later that at that point they didn't believe—that is literally what they said, "didn't believe"—the patient would survive.

I don't remember why—maybe it was the general bewilderment, or the commotion of those first dramatic minutes—but first they took the Holy Father up to the tenth floor, then down to the ninth floor, and only then to the operating room. And at a certain point, I heard someone shouting, "Let us go first!" It was the nurses, who were forcing open the two doors.

I was also allowed in. There were a lot of people. I was standing in a corner, so I was able to find out everything right away. There were problems with the Pope's blood pressure and his heart wasn't beating properly. But the worst moment was when Dr. Buzzonetti came up to ask me to give the Holy Father the last anointing. I did it immediately, but I was completely torn up inside. They might as well have told me that there wasn't anything more to be done for him. On top of that, the first blood transfusion hadn't worked. So they had to do a second one, and this time the doctors themselves had to donate the blood.

Fortunately, the surgeon, Professor Francesco Crucitti, was on the scene by this time. Since the principal surgeon was in Milan, Crucitti had volunteered to operate. And so he started the surgery.

At long last, it started! At this point, I was outside the operating room, and all I did was pray, pray, pray. From time to time, a doctor would come in to tell me how the operation was going, and then I would pray more intensely, abandoning myself into the hands of God and calling upon Our Lady.

After almost five and a half hours, someone—I don't remember his face, but I do remember what he said—came to tell me that the operation was over, that it had gone well, and that the prognosis was looking better for the Pope.

Next, they took the Holy Father to intensive care, where he came out of the anesthesia very early the next morning. He opened his eyes, looked at me for a long time as if he couldn't quite figure out who I was, and then spoke just a few words: "hurts . . . thirsty." And then: "just like Bachelet." I guess he had woken up thinking of a certain parallel with Professor Vittorio Bachelet, who had been assassinated by the Red Brigades the previous year.

The Pope slept for a while, then woke up in the early morning. He looked at me again, this time with full awareness, and, unbelievably, asked me if he had recited Compline. He thought it was still Wednesday, May 13.

The first three days were terrible. The Holy Father prayed continually. And he suffered. He suffered a lot. But he was suffering even more—with a constant, unrelenting interior pain—because Cardinal Wyszynski was on his deathbed.

I had seen the primate just two days before. He was in his Warsaw residence, bedridden with his final illness. The Holy Father had sent me expressly to pay him a visit. The cardinal knew that the end was imminent, but he was serene. He had abandoned himself completely into God's hands. We spoke for a long time. He asked me to convey his last wishes to the Holy Father. He also wrote him a letter.

But then, when he found out about the assassination attempt, and learned that the Holy Father was in danger of death, Wyszynski—how can I put this?—grabbed hold of life and refused to let go until he knew for certain. . . . And as a result, he endured no less than three weeks of terrible pain. He closed his eyes for the last time only after receiving confirmation that the Pope was out of danger.

I still get emotional when I recall the last short telephone conversation between the primate, who was dying, and the Pope, who was weak but on his way to recovery. You could hear the cardinal's feeble voice saying, "We're united in suffering . . . but you're okay." And then: "Holy Father, give me your blessing." And Wojtyla, though reluctant to pronounce the blessing, because he knew it would be their last good-bye, said, "Yes, of course. I bless your mouth. . . . I bless your hands."

But John Paul II wasn't out of the woods yet. Back in the Vatican, he came down with another fever, which was accompanied by a general malaise and increasingly acute pain. He was hospitalized again at Gemelli, where they finally discovered that he had cytomegalovirus. After he had recovered from the infection, he needed a second operation to get rid of the temporary colostomy. This time, everything went well, though, and there were no further complications. On August 14, the day before the Feast of the Assumption, the Holy Father was released for good from the hospital.

But now I need to take a step back. I need to say something about Fatima. . . .

Truth be told, John Paul II didn't think about Fatima at all in the days immediately following the assassination attempt. It was only later, after he had recovered and was getting back some of his old strength, that he started reflecting on what was, to say the least, an extraordinary coincidence. Two thirteenths of May! One in 1917, when the Virgin of Fatima appeared for the first time, and one in 1981, when they tried to kill him.

After pondering it for a while, the Pope finally requested to see the Third Secret. The Third Secret, which Mary had revealed to the three children when she appeared at Fatima, was kept in the archives of the Congregation for the Doctrine of the Faith. And on July 18, if I'm not mistaken, the then prefect, Cardinal Franjo Šeper, delivered two envelopes—one with Sister Lucia's original Portuguese text, and the other with the Italian translation—to Eduardo Martínez Somalo, the deputy secretary of state. Martínez Somalo then took the two envelopes to Gemelli.

This was during the second hospitalization. It was there, in the hospital, that the Holy Father read the "secret." When he was finished, all his remaining doubts were gone. In Sister Lucia's vision, he recognized his own destiny. He became convinced that his life had been saved—no, given back to him anew—thanks to Our Lady's intervention and protection.

It's true, of course, that the "bishop dressed in white" is killed in Sister Lucia's vision, whereas John Paul II escaped an almost certain death. So? Couldn't that have been the real point of the vision? Couldn't it have been trying to tell us that the paths of history, of human existence, are not necessarily fixed in advance? And that there is a Providence, a "motherly hand," which can intervene and cause a shooter, who is certain of hitting his target, to miss?

"One hand shot, and another guided the bullet" was how the Holy Father put it.

And today that bullet, made forever harmless, lies encased within the crown on Our Lady's statue in Fatima.

20.

But Who Armed the Killer?

"So why aren't you dead?" Mehmet Ali Agca asked.

That was a question John Paul II wasn't expecting to hear.

The Pope had decided to meet face-to-face with the man who tried to kill him. He wanted to repeat his words of forgiveness to his would-be killer in person. And he also wanted to give some meaning—a meaning Ali Agca could understand—to the gesture of Christian love he was performing. The first thing he said was, "Today we meet as men. No, as brothers."

But as he sat next to Ali Agca in a bare cell in the Rebibbia prison, inclining his head to hear the prisoner better, the Pope was surprised to hear the question: "So why aren't you dead?"

Perhaps Karol Wojtyla was also hoping that this meeting would help him understand why the man sitting next to him had tried to kill him. What he got instead was this strange question: "I know I was aiming right. I know that the bullet was a killer. So why aren't you dead?"

I wasn't directly present at the meeting. I was standing a few yards away. But my impression, or I suppose I should say my interpretation, is that Ali Agca was terrified by the fact that there were forces bigger than he was. The fact is that he had aimed well, and yet his victim was still alive. And so there were forces beyond his control, and he was terrified by them. Plus, he had found out that there wasn't just one Fatima—Mohammed's daughter—but another one, whom he called the "goddess of Fatima." And he himself said he was afraid that this powerful goddess would avenge herself on him and "get rid of him."

The whole meeting ended up revolving around that. And the Holy Father—as he himself would often recall with deep concern—never once heard the words *forgive me*.

"So why aren't you dead?" John Paul II never forgot that question. He carried it around with him for years, pondering it over and over again.

He had already come up with a first answer, the one that really counted, because it convinced him that Our Lady had saved him. But there was a second answer that had to be given, or at least attempted. And, as he was approaching the end of his life, he felt something like a need to communicate the conclusion he had reached about it.

In his last book, Memory and Identity, *we read these words: "Ali Agca, as everyone says, is a professional assassin. The shooting was not his initiative, someone else planned it, someone else commissioned him."*

At this point, one can't help wondering why the Pope finally broke so many years of silence. Was it because he had received some new information about who was behind the assassination attempt?

◆ ◆ ◆

Absolutely not! The fact is that the Holy Father always thought about everything in terms of faith. He used to say that even this trial had been a grace for him.

Now, as for the information . . . There's been a lot of talk about information supposedly relayed by secret service agencies from various countries. Well, I can tell you for a fact that it never got relayed to the Pope. And, as far as any tips are concerned, Cardinal Casaroli (the then secretary of state), Cardinal Silvestrini (at the time secretary of the Council for Public Affairs), and Cardinal Martínez Somalo (at the time deputy secretary of state) had already stated that they'd never received any.

Rumors? Of course. We would always hear a lot of rumors before every trip. But they were rumors you couldn't take seriously. And no one really believed them. Also because—as we used to ask—who could even think of trying to kill a Pope, a man of religion who travels the world preaching peace?

So the Holy Father reached the conclusions he reached not because he had any precise or specific information, but by a process of deduction. In other words, it seemed objectively impossible that Ali Agca could have been acting alone, or that he had done the whole thing by himself.

So the Pope thought it was a real plot. And that all the likely trails eventually pointed directly or indirectly to the KGB as the ultimate organizer.

Ali Agca was a perfect killer. Sent by someone who thought the Pope was dangerous and inconvenient. By someone who was afraid of John Paul II. By someone who'd been frightened, seriously frightened, as soon as they'd heard that a Polish Pope had been elected. And so it's natural to look to the Communist world, to suspect, at least hypothetically, that the KGB was behind whoever made the immediate decision.

It is an incontestable fact that Karol Wojtyla's election to the papacy dismayed a lot of people in the capitals of the Eastern-bloc countries. Just three weeks after the election, the Soviets had already prepared an initial analysis of its possible consequences for the Communist countries. A year later, there was a top secret document—signed by Mikhail Suslov, the chief ideologue of the Communist party, and approved by the entire Secretariat of the Central Committee, including Gorbachev—outlining a series of measures to counter the Polish Pope and his mission in the world.

Then there was John Paul II's first trip to Poland, which Brezhnev had personally worked to the very last minute to prevent. The following year, Solidarity, the first great workers' revolution in the Communist world, was born. And, as early as 1981, the more radical elements of Solidarity, whose mere existence had already dealt a deathblow to Marxist ideology, were becoming more and more openly hostile to the Soviets.

There was plenty to magnify the fears of the Communist bosses. And so to lend credence to the idea that the secret service, or at least crazed splinter groups within the secret service, decided to eliminate the Polish Pope, while perhaps leaving the practical implementation to others.

You have to keep in mind all the elements of the situation: the election of a Pope disliked by the Kremlin; his first trip to Poland as Pontiff; the explosion of Solidarity. On top of that, the Polish Church was losing its great primate, Cardinal Wyszynski, who was already at death's door. Look—doesn't everything point in that direction? Don't all roads, however disparate they are, lead to the KGB?

In fact, we never believed in the "Bulgarian connection," or in a lot of other hypotheses that were in circulation. Like the one that started up after the disappearance of Emanuela Orlandi, when the press, aided and abetted by a few conspiracy nuts, tried to float the theory that it was somehow connected with the assassination attempt, the Vatican, and the Pope. But there was no objective link, either direct or indirect. Really, all there was to it was the Holy Father's anxiety over the fate of that poor girl and his Christian solidarity with her suffering family.

But what would have happened if on May 13, 1981, the two shots fired from Ali Agca's 9mm Browning had actually hit their target?

I've wondered about that myself. What would have happened if Our Lady's hand hadn't deflected the bullet? What would the world's future have been like? The fact is that without the help of the Polish Pope, the Solidarity revolution would hardly have survived. And the history of Eastern Europe would probably have turned out differently, too.

But fate (or Providence, believers will say) wanted it otherwise. It decreed that Ali Agca would have to ask the man whom he had tried to shoot to death: "So why aren't you dead?"

But he never asked for forgiveness!

John Paul II had even written him a letter: "Dear brother, how could we appear before the sight of God if we do not forgive each other here on earth?"

In the end, the letter was never sent. Ali Agca would probably have exploited it. And the Holy Father preferred to visit him in person. He preferred to perform an act of forgiveness and to shake his would-be assassin's hand—of all hands!

But from Ali Agca himself, nothing. All he cared about were the revelations of Fatima. The only thing that interested him was figuring out who had prevented him from killing the Pope. But asking the Pope's forgiveness? Sorry, not interested!

And he never did it, either. He never asked for forgiveness!

21.

A Whole Nation
Behind Bars

The hands of the clock had just marked the beginning of the new day. It was Sunday, December 13, 1981. And the tanks could already be seen rolling through the main streets of Warsaw. Hours later, the West, thanks mainly to a few radio operators, started to get the first fragmentary news. The Vatican tried to make contact with Poland, but to no avail. The telephones were dead.

It was only later that we were able to figure out the reason for the silence. All channels of communication had already been cut before midnight. At the same time, all the borders had been closed. So, at first we had to rely on TV and radio, but then, after the official announcement at 6:00 A.M., we got more information as the morning wore on. And that's how we found out that martial law had been declared in Poland. It was a real shock.

Obviously, we were already frightened. And there had been a growing concern about a possible invasion in the days leading up to the declaration. Brzezinski had telephoned to say something to that effect. On top of that, we knew that the Warsaw Pact forces already stationed in Poland were heading toward the capital. But no one could believe that they would resort to martial law. Even the Holy Father was surprised when he found out—anguished and surprised.

At that point, thousands of union leaders and intellectuals had already been shipped off to internment camps and Lech Walesa, the leader of Solidarity, was being held at an undisclosed location. The imposition of martial law meant the suspension of union activities and the abolition of the right to work. First and foremost, though, it meant the abolition of an entire people's right to freedom.

It was a profound humiliation for Poland. After all that it had suffered throughout its history, Poland didn't deserve this new martyrdom. It didn't deserve to be punished so severely.

In some respects, what happened was the inevitable outcome of a crisis that had been growing worse with every passing month. The Polish Church—now under the leadership of the new primate, Cardinal Józef Glemp—had futilely tried to mediate between the two parties: Solidarity, whose more radical groups were more aggressively and openly anti-Soviet with every new day, and an increasingly militarized regime (after the nomination of General Wojciech Jaruzelski as secretary of the Communist party) that itself was under mounting pressure from Moscow.

Adam Michnik, one of the historic leaders of the Left, said that "the USSR has done everything to camouflage its involvement in the 'declaration.'" They put on an excellent show: "The Poles themselves have resolved their own problems." In fact, Jaruzelski opted for an internal coup as the "lesser of two evils."

◆ ◆ ◆

But it was the "lesser of two evils" for General Jaruzelski, as he would later try to explain. As it turned out, though, the whole world condemned his decision. And I am convinced that if the general had stood his ground against the pressures (or the blackmail, or even the bluff, according to some) coming from Moscow, the Soviet Union would never have intervened. They were already tragically bogged down in Afghanistan. And so at that point, how could they have invaded a country even bigger than Afghanistan and fought a war on two fronts?

Late in the morning of the thirteenth, John Paul, still deeply shaken, spoke to the faithful, using the word Solidarity six times. Then, turning to Our Lady, he "explained" to her—as if she, and not the Kremlin, were his interlocutor—various aspects of the Church's social teaching regarding justice.

This was the origin of the idea of praying to the Virgin of Czestochowa at the end of each of the Wednesday general audiences. The Pope would use this prayer as an opportunity to insist on the right of his fellow countrymen to live their own lives and to resolve their internal problems according to their own beliefs.

That evening after dinner, the Holy Father said to us, "Let's pray. Let's pray very calmly. And let's wait for a sign from on High." He was able to get through difficult times like these by entrusting himself completely to God and His divine Providence. Meanwhile, though, he was pondering what he could do to help his poor country.

It was clear that he couldn't go to Poland. In fact, he immediately ruled out the idea. But he did think it was important to give a visible sign of the Pope's and the Church's love for the Polish people. And so he decided to send Archbishop—today Cardinal—Luigi Poggi, who at the time was the apostolic nuncio in charge of special affairs, with a particular focus on Eastern Europe.

December 17 brought tragic news. Workers at the Wujek mine in Katowice went on strike and shut it down. The ZOMO— mechanized reserve forces known for their violence and propensity for cruelty—stepped in. There was a very violent clash. Nine workers were killed.

Pained by these deaths, the Pope immediately wrote to General Jaruzelski, appealing to him in conscience to put an end to "the spilling of Polish blood" and to return to the methods of peaceful dialogue that had characterized the quest for social renewal since August 1980. And the Pope preceded his appeal with the suggestion of an obvious parallel between martial law and the Nazi occupation.

A few short hours later, Jerzy Kuberski turned up at the Vatican. Kuberski was the minister of Religious Affairs, but, since the man in charge was absent, he was heading up the Polish government delegation to the Apostolic See. Kuberski was also the one who had contacted Cardinal Glemp at 5:00 A.M. on December 13 to inform him that martial law was to be declared an hour later.

Kuberski was received by Archbishop Achille Silvestrini, the secretary of the Church's Council of Public Affairs. He formally presented Silvestrini with Jaruzelski's demand that the Pope withdraw his letter. The general, Kuberski said, found the Pope's reference to Nazism completely unacceptable. Naturally, Sil-

vestrini very firmly replied that such a withdrawal was out of the question. He suggested that the general write directly to the Pontiff.

That was the end of the story for the Vatican. But afterward, the Pope must obviously have feared that the Nazi reference risked provoking the opposite of the basic and immediate goal of the letter, which was the prevention of any further killing. The reference to the Nazi invasion was thus dropped in favor of an allusion to the "grave offenses" that Poland had endured and the "great amounts of blood" that the people had spilled in the "last two centuries."

Archbishop Poggi set off with this new letter, which was dated December 18, 1981. He faced a journey fraught with problems and obstacles. Poggi flew to Vienna, and from there took the train to Poland. But he was stopped at the Czechoslovak border (the train sat on the tracks for an hour as the police searched the baggage) because he didn't have a transit visa for Czechoslovakia. Finally, he arrived in Warsaw, requested an interview with Jaruzelski, and, upon entering the room, handed him the Pope's message.

It was Christmas Eve. The Holy Father had a candle lit in the window of his study as a sign of hope. In the evening, he got to experience a bit of typical Polish warmth, exchanging holiday greetings and the traditional *oplatek*—an unleavened bread that is broken into little pieces for everyone to share—with a small crowd of Poles living in Rome and elsewhere in Italy.

But that Christmas and New Year's was a profoundly sad time for John Paul II. One of the most distressing things he had to deal with was the lack of news and the interruption of communications. Of course, he did manage from time to time to contact opposition leaders who were outside Poland, like Bohdan Cywinski, one of the first advisers to Solidarity. And sometimes he even had opportunities for indirect communication with opposition leaders sitting in Polish prisons, like Michnik, to whom he sent a Bible. He even managed to contact Walesa in this way.

The prisons, in fact, were still full. The only way out was into the courtroom. Martial law continued, while the regime alternated between apparent concessions and more rigid clampdowns. Behind it all, of course, was Moscow, which refused even the tiniest opening. The Pope wasn't permitted to go to Czestochowa for the Marian celebrations in August 1982. Then, in October of the same year, the government officially disbanded Solidarity.

So it became necessary to find ways to to keep Solidarity alive, or at least to ensure the survival of its ideals, its revolutionary utopia.

At that point, the free world finally realized what was at stake. Everybody mobilized, putting aside ideological differences, conflict, and rivalry. States, international organizations, unions, volunteer groups, private charity and public assistance—all of it flowed into a huge outpouring of support that often reached Poland in unexpected ways. But however it got there, it was decisive for the survival of Solidarity.

Some of the Western media made certain insinuations about the help offered by the Apostolic See. Well, let me repeat here what I've already said before. John Paul II was never a financial or economic backer of Solidarity. He was a big moral backer of the union—and that's it. The Holy Father supported man's right to struggle for his own freedom and independence. So all the chatter about the Pope's supposed financial support for Solidarity is pure fiction. Actually, it's a downright lie.

Seemingly, then, Solidarity was finished. There had been a brief, yet thrilling, outbreak of freedom and unity, but the authorities had ground it into the dust.

And yet, the story didn't end. It couldn't. For one thing, the Polish regime, which was increasingly hated, and, therefore, increasingly isolated and weak, had to deal with an acute economic crisis due to the suspension of Western economic aid.

So the Communist bosses couldn't afford not to reestablish some sort of dialogue with the Church. Jaruzelski and Cardinal Glemp met. The meeting made it possible to set a date for the second papal visit.

And, thanks to these new developments, things began to happen. Walesa was freed from house arrest in Arlamowo. Most of the internment camps were shut down. Nevertheless, the restrictions on individual and civil liberties remained in effect; the special tribunals were still in operation; and there was still a heavy climate of oppression and uncertainty. Poles felt deprived of air—of the air that they had breathed freely in the Solidarity days.

But John Paul II's visit to Poland was approaching.

22.

Solidarity Lives!

John Paul II was absolutely determined to go back to Poland. He felt it was his duty to help the Polish people recover their self-confidence and their will to hope, if nothing else.

But could he go to Poland under martial law? Wouldn't he end up legitimating the situation without intending to? In a word, was it better to shake hands with the dictators or to refuse to go to Poland altogether?

Finally, after much reflection, the Pope hit upon the most logical answer: Yes, he could go—but he would clearly convey his disapproval of the current state of affairs.

This proved to be a just, wise, and effective decision. Because it was the only way to save Solidarity and Lech Walesa.

But it's best to begin at the beginning.

I'll try to recall the main highlights of this June 1983 trip, which decided the future of Poland. I'll try to do it partly on the basis of my notes and partly relying on my memory.

At that point, Walesa didn't exist as far as the Communist leaders were concerned. They didn't even mention his name.

When they had to talk about him, they simply called him "the electrician." Now, this is exactly why the Pope made it known that he would go to Poland only on the condition that he could meet with Walesa. But General Jaruzelski was resolutely against any such meeting. And so, in order to get beyond the impasse, they worked out a compromise. It was a pretty flimsy one, though. A lot was still up in the air, or was left implicit, and many of the details were still vague.

In fact, when the Holy Father arrived in Poland on June 16, he discovered that the meeting was not at all certain, and that it actually might fall through. He vented his dismay with his closest collaborators. "If I can't see him, then I'm going back to Rome!" Some of his entourage raised objections, but his answer was simply, "I have to be consistent in the eyes of the people!"

One thing was certain: He made known his intention to back Solidarity as soon as he got off the plane. He kissed the ground—though he had already done that on his first visit—and explained that he felt as if he were kissing a mother bowed down by new afflictions. He added that he was coming for everyone, including those who were in prison. Then, at Cardinal Wyszynski's tomb in the cathedral, he thanked Providence for sparing him the painful events of December 13, 1981. That didn't make it into the newspapers the next day.

The next step was the meeting with General Jaruzelski. In his public speech, the Pope expressly demanded the implementation of the agreements signed by union leaders and the government in August 1980. In the private interview, he essentially told the general that, while he might even understand the decision to introduce martial law, he absolutely couldn't understand the abolition of Solidarity, because it was an expression of the soul of Poland.

On the way back from the interview, John Paul II stopped in the Capuchin church, where they preserve the heart of one of the great kings of Poland, Jan Sobieski. And there he had an opportunity to speak with several members of the opposition, mainly intellectuals and artists, as well as with the mother of a young man killed by the police.

The next stop was Czestochowa. All of a sudden, the tension visibly escalated. The police were on the alert because of the huge turnout of young people. And yet, despite the young people's burning enthusiasm, and their obvious desire to turn the meeting into a demonstration against the regime, the Pope nipped any type of protest in the bud. At the same time, his injunction—"You've got to be vigilant!"—was certainly understood as more than mere rhetoric.

The following day, Sunday, June 19, there was a Marian celebration, with Mass and the crowning of four images of the Virgin from four different shrines. There was an incredible crowd of two million people, and in his homily John Paul II expressly stated that Poland should be sovereign and that sovereignty is based on the liberties of the citizenry.

At around the same time, a few politburo men showed up in Czestochowa. They were already deeply disturbed by the Pope's statements, but they were even more concerned about what he might say in his "solemn appeal," which was planned for that evening. They asked for an interview with Bronislaw Dabrowski, the secretary of the Polish Bishops' Conference, and told him in no uncertain terms that the Pope would have to alter the message of his speeches.

Archbishop Dabrowski conveyed this to the Pope and then went back to the Party representatives with the Pope's answer. John Paul II replied that if he couldn't say what he thought, if he couldn't speak freely in his own country, then he would go back to Rome!

Confronted with John Paul II's firm resolution, the Party leaders made no answer, but went home to Warsaw to file their report. For his part, the Holy Father did make a few minor adjustments in his appeal, but they only affected its tone, not its ideas and arguments. Among other things, he called for renewed, courageous dialogue on social issues. Which was exactly what Jaruzelski had insisted—even to the Pope's face—he wouldn't accept.

The Pope went on to Poznań, where he explicitly mentioned Solidarity for the first time on the trip. In Katowice, he asserted the workers' right to form unions without government interference. In Wroclaw, he stressed the importance of retaining everything positive about Solidarity. Meanwhile, the altar boys were pulling up his white tunic to reveal the now world-famous T-shirt with the red letters.

On the evening of August 21, John Paul II reached Kraków. They wanted him to use a closed vehicle instead of the Popemobile, but he declined the offer. Instead, he drove through the city in a bus. He arrived at the archbishop's residence and sat down to dinner, but he had to get up from his meal and go to the window to talk with thousands of young people who had gathered to greet him. This time, too, certain members of the papal entourage began to worry and to say that he should be more "contained."

The following day, two million people thronged Blonie Park for the beatification of two great Poles: Father Raphael Kalinowski, a Carmelite, and Brother Albert Chmielowski, the founder of the Albertine Brothers and Sisters, who spent his life serving the world's humblest. As the crowd was slowly breaking up after Mass, the Solidarity banners were unfurled. At that point, helicopters flew just above the heads of the people. They were obviously trying to frighten the crowd and disperse them. But it didn't work. Instead, everything proceeded in a quiet and orderly fashion, just as the Holy Father wished, without even the smallest hint of a provocation.

Meanwhile, however, the regime was terrified. That afternoon, there was a second unexpected meeting between the Pope and General Jaruzelski on the Wawel Hill. Contrary to what the spin doctors later asserted, it was the government, and not the Church, that called for the meeting. The purpose was partly to calm things down a bit, partly to dampen the impact of the next day's event, and partly to give Jaruzelski a chance to explain, as he put it, "his" position to the Pope—which might be the reason why the interview dragged on for ninety minutes.

In the Holy Father's eyes, if I may be allowed to interpret his thoughts a bit, the general was an intelligent and cultured man, who, in his own way, was even something of a patriot. The problem was that politically he looked eastward, not westward. In other words, when it came to the future of Poland, Jaruzelski still saw every possible outcome in terms of Moscow, and never of the West.

Although the Pope's meeting with Lech Walesa had been kept a secret until the last minute, it finally took place on the morning of June 23. Walesa, along with his wife and four of his children, was flown in by helicopter. The place—which the regime had chosen because it was so remote—was a mountain retreat near Zakopane, on the slopes of the Tatras. The secret service had prepared everything on the spot, hiding microphones all over the room and replacing the usual waiters with their own trained specialists.

The whole thing was so obviously rigged, though, that the Holy Father immediately realized what was going on. He took Walesa into the hallway and invited him to sit down on a bench. It was possible bugs had been placed there, too. And yet, even if their conversation were overheard, there would be no harm done. It was no big deal.

The important thing at that point wasn't what the Pope and Walesa might say, but the fact of their meeting itself. The important thing was that John Paul II was there with Walesa. "All I wanted to tell you was this: I pray for you every day." That is, he prayed every day for Walesa and for all the men and women of Solidarity. By meeting with Walesa, the Pope showed the whole world, starting with the Communist bosses, that the movement was alive and that the story was by no means over.

This explains the quick decision to belie an imprudent article in *L'Osservatore Romano* that interpreted the meeting with Walesa as a kind of farewell to arms for a defeated soldier, as if Walesa and Solidarity had been finally beaten in their struggle with the regime! But how could we allow even the suggestion that the Church had abandoned Solidarity? How could we let people think that the Church wasn't a reliable and dependable partner of the working class?

The trip ended with a remarkable line from Jablonski, the president of the Council of State. In a private meeting, Jablonski addressed John Paul II with these words: "On his arrival, we greeted the Pope of peace; in four years we will greet the Pope of reconciliation." I'm not sure that General Jaruzelski was completely in agreement with Jablonski's judgment.

Anyway, the trip went well, in spite of the difficulties. The Holy Father found the right way to support a sad, disappointed, and embittered nation and to keep Solidarity alive, despite its of-

ficial nonexistence. And he managed to do that without even in-
voluntarily provoking disorder or conflict.

*A month later, Jaruzelski lifted martial law and began to empty
the prisons. He thus managed to give the regime a certain semblance of liberality.*

*Nevertheless, years would go by before Poland could go back
to being a free country. They would be years full of contradiction,
like all periods of transition: years full of both dark shadows and
bright lights of hope. The year 1984 brought the gruesome assassination of Father Jerzy Popieluszko, a courageous priest and
strong backer of Solidarity and workers' rights. Then, in 1987,
John Paul II returned to Poland for the third time.*

*This trip was, in his own words, a "service of truth," a denun-
ciation of the stagnation that by now was the trademark of "real
socialism." It launched a tide of events that, within two years,
would bring freedom, the relegalization of Solidarity, the first
non-Communist postwar government in Eastern Europe—
headed by a Catholic, Tadeusz Mazowiecki—and, finally, in
1990, the presidency of the ex-electrician of the Lenin Shipyard.*

*In a word, Poland was the forerunner of the great turnaround
that marked the end of communism.*

23.

A New Evangelization

It was only toward the end of the pontificate that the Vatican watchers began to take note. They discovered that for the first time since the Counter-Reformation, the Church was beginning to declericalize itself. The Second Vatican Council laid the groundwork for this process, but it never really got off the ground—that is, not until John Paul II gave it a new start. The moment had come to dismantle—as he himself put it—"the old one-sided emphasis on the clergy."

He was a man of the council. He always went back to the council for guidance in planning the next steps in the Church's life and mission. And the council was his inspiration for gradually introducing the idea that the Church is a communion, in fact, a family, where all the baptized have an equal dignity, so that no one should feel marginalized or, worse, excluded. He thus succeeded in giving an increasingly higher profile to charisms, the laity, and community, rather than simply reasserting the institutional, the clergy, and the hierarchy. As a result, new protagonists came into the spotlight: the young, women, and the ecclesial movements.

The process was initiated by the Encyclical Redemptor Hominis, *which was followed up by* Dives in Misericordia *and* Dominum et Vivificantem. *And this trilogy—which in fact anticipated the program of the pontificate—led to a renewed proclamation of the Trinitarian dimension of faith (and so to a new emphasis on what is distinctively Christian). It also a fostered a new proclamation of the Trinitarian meaning of the Church (and thus of its nature, mission, and even its structure). The Pope was telling us, in other words, that, as a reflection of the mystery of the Trinity, the Church is called to manifest more and more its deep nature as a harmonious interplay of unity and multiplicity, of identity and difference.*

The first three encyclicals were the ones that underscored this image of the Church as a communion that is enfleshed in the heart of human history. They presented a Church whose essential mission is to proclaim God's love, mercy, and forgiveness.

Though this idea was obviously anchored in Vatican II, it didn't begin there. Anyone who had followed Karol Wojtyla's theological and pastoral journey as priest and bishop would have noticed that his mind, his plans, and his goals had always been full of the conception of the Church we've been talking about.

I would say that he had a kind of inspiration, almost a vision, which he then proceeded to implement wherever he found himself in a leadership role in the Church. And he did the same thing throughout his pontificate, too. As Pope, he moved straight ahead without hesitation.

◆   ◆   ◆

It is indeed surprising, to say the least, how soon after his election John Paul II was able to relativize, or at least to reduce, the postconciliar conflict between conservatives and progressives. He thus showed that none of the crises afflicting the Church was beyond resolution. And, by the same token, he helped the Church get beyond the palpable sense of discouragement, of resignation, and even of "darkened hope," as he once put it, that lingered at the end of the 1970s.

Once that had happened, the Pope could commit the whole Catholic body to a vast work of renewal, which translated into a growth in spirituality, witness, engagement, and presence in the world. Above all, though, this commitment to renewal ripened into a great plan for evangelization that was no longer confined only to the traditional mission countries, but was also addressed to a Western world increasingly sunk in spiritual amnesia.

Yes, that was the origin of the "new evangelization," which ended up becoming one of the hallmarks of John Paul II's pontificate. The idea came to him when he noticed—especially during the trips—that there was a really urgent need to reinvigorate the churches in the old Christian countries. He thought this was particularly true of Europe, because the Continent was gradually drifting further and further from its roots, and so from its history and culture. He thus believed it was necessary to go back to the sources of the faith in order to give the mission of evangelization new dynamism and impact.

This task is a duty of the first importance, and it's incumbent upon the Church and on all Christians, who are called to evangelize wherever they happen to be living out their lives at the moment. But it wasn't just a duty for Karol Wojtyla, who had a predisposition to what I like to call "Gospel freshness." In other words, he always tried to start the renewal process with himself. His main method was reading the Gospel. He read Holy Scripture daily until the very end of his life. It was Scripture that constantly reignited his great impatience to spread Christ's message around the world. To spread the message and, at the same time, to strengthen faith where it already existed.

Every other commitment, for example to peace and justice, always had a spiritual and religious motivation—that is, it was always based on faith and the Gospel. Otherwise, the Church would boil down in the end to a big social agency or an international aid organization.

So you could say that John Paul II's entire pontificate was a continual implementation of Vatican II.

Part of the reason for that was that he always went back to certain conciliar documents as reference points for his mission. The ones on the laity, on ecumenism, or on religious freedom are examples that come to mind. His main reference point, though, was the Pastoral Constitution *Gaudium et Spes,* which he had helped to write. It guided him in his efforts to make the Church more visible and influential in society—in the sense of bearing witness, being a leaven of the Gospel, and serving man.

The second part of Gaudium et Spes *deals with five areas: the family, culture, social and economic life, politics, and peace and the community of peoples. In each of these domains, John Paul II took the thinking of Vatican II considerably further.*

✦ ✦ ✦

Culture, for instance, was one of Karol Wojtyla's big interests. Just think of his yearly meetings with scientists and philosophers at Castel Gandolfo. For him, those meetings were a chance for dialogue and debate, but they also gave him the opportunity to become informed about the latest developments in human thought, and, most important, to verify whether they did or didn't serve man and human dignity.

That's really the point, I think: Culture is the basis of the integral development of the person. John Paul II believed culture makes man be more himself; it enables him to be more human. And culture is the root of the principles and values that define the ethos of a people and the norms by which a society lives. And it's in culture, hence in memory, that every nation can find its origin, but also the means to defend its own identity and sovereignty. We've already seen that Poland was able to do this in the long, painful years of foreign partitions and occupations.

The Pope chose to say all this in the most secular of possible cultural contexts: UNESCO. Later, he reaffirmed the same message in Fides et Ratio. His argument was that the positive encounter between faith and culture offers a real alternative to the materialism and injustice of a world without ethical moorings.

What is more, he had already put his money where his mouth was by reopening the Galileo affair. The reexamination of the case not only led to an admission that the condemnation of Galileo was a mistake but also signaled a new attitude toward scientific research on the part of the Church.

✦ ✦ ✦

At this point, I think the accusations leveled against John Paul II completely collapse under their own weight. Especially the charge that he tried to freeze—or worse, bury—Vatican II.

All you have to do is read his will to realize that he was always faithful to the Council and that even at the end of his life, the Council was at the center of his mission. It was a commitment that he bequeathed as a kind of legacy to the generations coming after him. He was speaking to them when he wrote: "I am convinced that it will long be granted to the new generations to draw from the treasures that this 20th-century Council has lavished upon us."

24.

Youth, Women, and the Ecclesial Movements

There was an immediate rapport between John Paul II and the youth.

"You are my hope," the Pope told them at the beginning of his pontificate. He didn't just say that because it sounded good. He said it because he believed it. Even as a newly minted priest, he had started learning how to relate to young people, how to understand their problems, their contradictions, their reasons for questioning religion and the Church, and their impatience to change society.

For their part, the young people initially looked at the new Pope with curiosity, but they eventually took to him with growing affection. They still had left over from the 1960s something of an antipathy to any sort of authority or religious belief. But the Pope was a magnet for them. When he bore witness to his beliefs, he was credible. And he was like a father, not only spiritually but emotionally, as well.

Everything might have stayed as it was in that initial phase of mutual interest. But at the end of May 1980, the Pope went to

Paris, where he met with thousands of young people in the Parc des Princes stadium. He talked with them for three hours: They asked real, tough questions, and he gave them straight, honest answers.

Just as the Mexico trip was the first of many, many journeys, the meeting in the Parc des Princes was the first step in a dialogue between the Church and the younger generation.

That day in Paris convinced the Pope that young people were willing to share his journey to Christ. And it reinforced his plans to proclaim a reinvigorated, fresh faith and his intuition that there was work for a pastor to do among young people.

And the youth began to identify with the spiritual, moral, and human values that the Holy Father was proposing to them. They appreciated his way of dialoguing. He was demanding, but also convincing, because he was motivated by love for them.

The meeting in the Parc des Princes was also the origin of World Youth Day. The Pope invited young people to Rome for the Holy Year of the Redemption (1983) and for the International Year of Youth declared by the United Nations in 1985. At that point, young people all over the world began to feel the need to continue these meetings with the Pope. They had a need to hear the words of a Pope who didn't make concessions or water down the truths of Christianity, but helped them in their quest for God, for the real meaning of morality, for the difference between good and evil. They needed to hear the words that others—family members, teachers, authorities, and sometimes even priests—weren't telling them.

◆   ◆   ◆

The result was a huge movement of young people behind the Cross, which he commissioned them to carry through the streets of the world, proclaiming Christ crucified, but also Christ risen. And it was the Pope who inspired them.

So the Pope helped the youth rediscover love for Christ, and so relearn the joy of being young and Christian. By the same token, he freed them from their complexes about being Catholic. It was the same thing he was trying to do with the Catholic world at large: free Catholics from the complexes that made them confine their faith to the sacristy.

It might seem unbelievable, but the people who at first had the most trouble dealing with all this were the bishops. For example, the American bishops didn't believe the 1993 World Youth Day in Denver would work, and the French bishops were sure the 1997 World Youth Day in Paris would be a failure. They thought the influence of secularism in their respective countries was so huge that an event of this nature could never succeed.

All the major newspapers were predicting that the meeting in Denver would be a resounding failure. Even the bishops seemed doubtful, if not actually afraid. Well, what happened is that they were expecting 200,000 young people at the most, but 700,000, and maybe even more, showed up.

And you had all these young Americans, these children of modernity and technology, resonating with the Pope's passionate appeal: "Don't be afraid to show yourselves in the streets and in public places!" He challenged them to become like the first apostles who preached Christ and his message of salvation in the city squares and the villages. "It's not the time to be ashamed of the Gospel, but to preach it out loud."

It was a memorable event. It also gave the bishops new courage and helped get the Catholic youth ministry off the ground.

There were also a lot of doubts regarding Paris, not only on the part of the bishops but even on the part of certain big names in the Roman Curia. But the outcome vindicated the courage of Cardinal Lustiger, the then archbishop of Paris, who had done all he could to make the event happen. Everybody was amazed by what a huge success it was. It was then, in fact, that people started saying that a new springtime was coming for the Church in France.

The cumulative effect of the World Youth Days was to re-awaken faith in a big way among young people, and not only among them. But we can't forget that each of these events has its own amazing, unique history.

One World Youth Day whose memory the Holy Father particularly treasured was the one at Jasna Góra in 1991. The Berlin Wall had fallen just a couple of years before. And so right under the eyes of Our Lady, you had young people from the Old World meeting their counterparts who had emerged from Communist oppression. And the meeting was a surprise for both sides. The young people from the West discovered the fresh faith of their Eastern European contemporaries. Meanwhile, the Eastern Europeans discovered that the West, too, was full of a living, socially engaged faith. So Jasna Góra cemented unity among the young on a global scale.

The high point, though, was probably the meeting at Tor Vergata for the Great Jubilee in 2000, when John Paul II exhorted a crowd of two million young people, saying, "Don't be afraid to be saints!"

◆   ◆   ◆

And now we come to a second group of people whom the Pope began to engage in dialogue: women. Like the youth, they were taking on a new role in the Church. For the Church had become less clerical and was starting to reflect—weakly at first, but that was definitely changing—the feminine side of God, which better expressed and embodied his mercy, his tenderness, in a word, His "motherhood."

Ever since he was a boy, Karol Wojtyla's heart was saturated with a feeling that was characteristic of his people and its traditions. I mean a great respect for, and consideration of, women, especially women who were mothers. In the world at large, though, he saw the opposite tendency gaining ground: serious disrespect for women, to the point of regarding them as objects of enjoyment and pleasure. Well, all of that reinforced the Pope's determination to help women to recover their dignity and to acknowledge their specific role in society and the life of the Church.

Pope John Paul II turned this "respect" and "consideration" into the Apostolic Letter Mulieris Dignitatem, *which reads like a paean to women.*

Mulieris Dignitatem was just one of many expressions of that attitude. Let me point out that the Holy Father showed it first of all in his behavior, in his gestures of tenderness toward women. There were so many trips, so many meetings, where he manifested that.

✦ ✦ ✦

In Mulieris Dignitatem, the Pope recalled a truth that is as old as Christianity itself but that was subsequently forgotten, ignored, or at least only very partially embodied in the life of the Church. I mean, of course, the fact that Christ promoted the dignity of women in a way that amounted to an extraordinary revolution, especially considering the times when He lived.

Feminism was one reading of what women are. In its wake, the Holy Father felt the need to offer a new reading. Let me put it like this: He wanted to look at what it means to be a woman with new eyes, in the light of faith, especially of Jesus' own behavior. Think of the way the Pope redefined the dignity of women in relation to men. Of course, he was just reaffirming what it says in Genesis about the equality of men and women. But he was also correcting centuries-old misinterpretations of the idea of submission: We have to understand that it's not just the woman who submits to man, but that both "mutually submit" to each other.

Next came the "Letter to Women," which solemnly acknowledged the "genius" or specific charism of women, of their vocation, and of the mission they are called to carry out in the Church as women.

Once the initial polemics were over, a lot of feminists, including some of the most radical ones, later thanked the Pope for the picture he had drawn of what it is to be a woman. He believed women have an identity of their own that isn't just a copy of what men do, but that they also possess specific rights and needs that society has to guarantee and protect.

And yet, the biggest protests against the Pope came precisely

from women, especially on the issue of women's ordination. For
example, on his 1979 trip to the United States, during a meet-
ing with women belonging to religious orders, Sister Theresa
Kane unexpectedly demanded that he "include women in all of
the Church's ministries."

On that occasion, as on other similar ones, the Pope always respected the individuals raising the questions and tried to understand their ideas. But he never failed to reiterate the Church's
position on women's ordination, as he did when they confronted
him about it that time in Washington. He said: Jesus Christ
could have done it differently, but He didn't. And we have to remain faithful to what Jesus said and did.

Today, women are more involved in Church life than at any other
time since the first century A.D. All around the world, more lay
and religious women than ever before carry out functions that
were once the exclusive preserve of priests and lay men. For the
first time in history, whole sectors of Church activity, like cate-
chesis and charitable outreach, belong almost exclusively to
women. And yet, John Paul II still felt compelled to appeal to the
Church community to eliminate every form of discrimination
against women.

Every revolution, big or small, requires a change of mentality,
and even before that, a change of heart, in order to overcome
whatever resistance there might be to the new situation. I should
also point out, though, that John Paul II opened up more and
more space for women in the Church. For example, he enabled
them to participate in synods and international conferences (in
Beijing, fourteen of the twenty-two members of the delegation

from the Holy See were women; plus, the head of the delegation was a woman, Mary Anne Glendon, who is also president of the Pontifical Academy of Social Sciences). Another thing he did was to try to place more women in the curial dicasteries (like Sister Enrica Rosanna, who is the undersecretary of the Congregation for Institutes of Consecrated Life and Societies of Apostolic Life). He also increased the number of his meetings with the general chapters of religious orders.

Finally, we need to say something about the ecclesial movements, which are perhaps the biggest innovation in contemporary Catholicism, both in terms of their active involvement in the Church and of the aid they give to the Pope's mission. In fact, we'd have to say that there has never been a flowering like this before, at least with respect to the number, variety, and relevance of the movements.

Karol Wojtyla had the opportunity to get to know the new movements as archbishop of Kraków. At the time, though, the only thing on his mind was how to defend them, since the Marxist regime feared the movements and was trying to wipe them out. One target was Light and Life. Its founder, Franciszek Blachnicki, spent time both in a Nazi concentration camp and in Communist prisons before dying in exile.

Then, as Pope, Karol Wojtyla was able to see the value of the movements, guide them toward maturity in the Church, and gradually give them a role in the mission of evangelization. He always said that they are a great gift of the Holy Spirit. The reason, he would explain, is that at the very moment when the post–Vatican II Church was in crisis, the Spirit gave it the movements, which filled the void of spirituality and missionary initiative. It was the same thing that happened, *mutatis mutandis* (with the necessary changes), with the medieval monks.

Some of the movements came into being during or immediately after World War II. Others were awakened by the Council or flourished in the climate of conciliar renewal.

The focus of the movements varies: a fresh new proposal of Catholic identity (Communion and Liberation); a spiritual experience modeled on the primitive Christian community (the Neocatechumenatal Way); interreligious dialogue as a privileged way to peace (the Community of Sant'Egidio and Focolare, though each pursues this dialogue in conjunction with other goals); personal piety and interiority later giving way to different types of social engagement (the Charismatic Renewal).

The Holy Father always managed to keep track of what the movements were doing and how they were developing, mainly because he was in frequent contact with many of the founders. He knew them well and he was very much on the same spiritual wavelength as they were. As examples, let me mention Don Luigi Giussani (who died just a few weeks before John Paul II), Chiara Lubich, Kiko Argüello and Carmen Hernández, Andrea Riccardi, Jean Vanier, and so many others.

For much the same reasons, the Pope appreciated Opus Dei's commitment to the lay apostolate. And, of course, he always set great store by Catholic Action, because it was rooted in the parishes, and he hoped that it would keep on developing its traditional role in the formation of laypeople in the Church.

The Pope met with the ecclesial movements in Rome on Pentecost in 1998. The meeting was an important acknowledgment of this

new reality in the Church. And while John Paul II appealed to the
movements to rise above any sort of competition or elitism, he al-
ways defended them and protected their autonomy and freedom
from pressures that might come from the Curia or the bishops.

Well, that may be something of an exaggeration. But it is true that
even when some bishops complained of conflicts with this or that
movement, or when correction was in order, John Paul II would,
of course, intervene, but he always tried to approach things with
a positive attitude, with trust. He supported all the movements—
all the healthy ones, of course, and without undermining the importance of the parish—because he saw them both as a pastoral
powerhouse and as a big source of priestly vocations.

He never thought that the movements posed a threat or worried that they might lead to sectarianism or, worse, to the dis-
memberment of the Church community.

Obviously it's still too early to make a final judgment that would
allow us to put aside once and for all the doubts and fears that
still remain. But it is a fact that thanks to the movements, the
Catholic Church is acquiring a new look, as it were.

There has certainly been a spiritual reawakening. And this
reawakening has led to the birth of new forms of apostolic and
social engagement. The result is that today we can bring the
Gospel to places we could never reach before, especially among
the young.

And there is hope, as John Paul II would always say, that, as
the movements continue to mature, they will foster the formation of adult Christians who are true witnesses of the faith in all
areas of society: the family, culture, and politics.

25.

"God's Sister" Teresa

One day in February 1986, Pope John Paul II visited the Nirmal Hriday Ashram, the Home for the Dying, in Calcutta. Accompanied by Mother Teresa, he visited the bedsides of dying men and women. He fed lepers and gave them water. As he left the building, he was visibly moved and upset. Then, on the pavement in front of the house, he hugged Mother Teresa tightly, as if to thank all the Missionaries of Charity for their extraordinary witness of love. And the nun seemed even smaller, like a little bird, in the Pope's arms.

Someone who was standing close by told me that the Holy Father whispered to Mother Teresa, "If I could, I would make this my headquarters as Pope." I didn't want to be indelicate, so I never asked the Pope if he had actually said that. But, as I think back on it, it has the ring of truth. After all, he was deeply moved at seeing Christ crucified in the suffering flesh of the poor. And, seeing Mother Teresa in the concrete setting of her daily life and mission, he realized once again that the absolute gratuity of self-giving is man's way to his deepest happiness. And Mother Teresa was a happy woman.

◆   ◆   ◆

There was indeed a deep bond between Mother Teresa and Karol Wojtyla. Although they came from different backgrounds, both were contemplatives whose mysticism was the catalyst for involvement in charitable, social, and apostolic work. Mother Teresa plunged into the world of the Calcutta slums in order to dedicate herself to the lepers and the dying. Karol Wojtyla lived through war and two systems of totalitarian oppression. The two shared a living witness to the unique value of every human person, even if he is at the very bottom of the social ladder.

Moreover, they were witnesses who knew how to use the symbolism of concrete, often bold, gestures that contemporary people could understand, even if those people weren't Christians or believers.

So, yes, they had a kind of spiritual kinship, as you would expect from two people who were totally in love with God. And this kinship became the basis of a strong friendship and a mutual understanding that didn't need a lot of words. They understood each other intuitively.

Their acquaintance dated back to the beginning of the 1970s, but it was cemented after Karol Wojtyla's election to the papacy. Whenever she came to Rome, Mother Teresa would let me know and would come visit the Holy Father. She would always tell him about the expansion of the Missionaries of Charity and the new houses that she was able to open in countries such as Russia that were still otherwise totally closed to the Catholic Church.

In some respects, Mother Teresa was a kind of mirror of John Paul II. Her mission embodied the essential goals of Wojtyla's

pontificate, such as the defense of life and the family, the pro-
tection of human rights, especially the rights of the humblest,
and the promotion of the dignity of women. When Mother
Teresa was awarded the Nobel Peace Prize—which she accepted
"in the name of the child who was never born"—the Pope asked
her to be a roving ambassador for life. "Go and say that every-
where. And speak in my name in the places where I cannot go."

Truth be told, Mother Teresa was hesitant at the beginning. She
said that the mission the Pope had entrusted to her was more
than she could handle. Very quickly, though, she showed her
true grit, if you'll pardon the expression, and became a real apostle of life. She went all over the world, proclaiming the dignity of
the human person and the defense of life, from conception to
natural death. And the Holy Father was grateful for the way she
threw herself into this mission and for the courage with which
she carried it out.

One day in the summer of 1982, she unexpectedly showed up
at Castel Gandolfo to ask John Paul II's blessing before leaving
for Lebanon. I brought her in to see the Holy Father, who was
just then receiving a group of young people. He asked her to sit
next to him and expained to the kids that she was going to a
country torn by civil war.

Mother Teresa left carrying a candle with an image of Our
Lady on top. When she arrived in Beirut, she obtained a cease-
fire for as long as the candle remained lit. This gave her the
chance to get about seventy handicapped children, most of them
Muslims, to safety.

By the time of her death, many people had already begun to see
her as a saint, including Hindus and Muslims. Toward the end

of her life, she got wind of these rumors, but she never paid much attention to them. She had gradually come to the conviction that holiness wasn't a luxury reserved for a few privileged souls, but was open to everyone. Holiness was simply a matter of doing the will of God in one's daily life.

The Holy Father was deeply saddened by her death. He said, "She's left us all a little orphaned." He said she was a real "sister of God," just as Saint Albert Chmielowski was a "brother of Our Lord." On the evening he received the news, he frankly expressed his hope that she would quickly be made a saint.

In fact, less than two years after Mother Teresa's death, he okayed the start of the beatification process. He also put the proceedings on the fast track. He didn't force anything, though, because he was convinced that she was a saint. Plus, no one could ignore the fact that her witness had cut across ideological, cultural, and religious divisions and had won over the whole world.

And I've no doubt that he was happy, in a spiritual sense, that he was able to raise to the glory of the altars a woman like Teresa, whom he had known personally. The same goes for Padre Pio, whom he had seen for Confession as a young priest (but without hearing any predictions about his future election to the papacy). Some of his canonizations were of saints who were almost as dear to him as family members, like Father Maximilian Kolbe, the martyr of love, or Faustina Kowalska, the Apostle of the Divine Mercy, or who had had an impact on his life, like Sister Teresa Benedicta of the Cross, aka Edith Stein, who was killed at Auschwitz.

John Paul II took seriously, if we can put it that way, Vatican II's teaching about the universal call to holiness. During his pontifi-

cate, there were 1,345 beatifications and 483 canonizations. And yet that was precisely one of the innovations for which he was often criticized and challenged. There was talk of an "inflation" of sanctity or of a "saint factory."

It was the council itself, though, that called everybody back to this high standard of Christian life. And so everyone—I repeat, everyone—can become a saint, even in the most normal and humble circumstances of life. I should also point out that Paul VI had already decided to streamline the canonization procedure. That said, it's certainly true that a very large number of people were canonized and beatified during John Paul II's pontificate— which, let's not forget, was an extraordinarily long one.

Anyway, the Holy Father once responded to one of his critics with a quip: "It's the Holy Spirit's fault." The thing is, though, that it actually wasn't just a quip.

The Church has become present everywhere, and the Gospel has reached the remotest places on the planet. So you'd expect the Christian message to have sunk its roots and borne fruit in all kinds of new settings. The beatifications reflect the action of the Holy Spirit; they're the most visible sign that the young churches in particular have attained a certain spiritual maturity.

For a long time, in fact, holiness seemed to be the monopoly of the churches evangelized in the early centuries, and, within those churches, of clerics, and even more of those belonging to religious orders.

John Paul II wanted the peoples of every nation to have blesseds and saints of their own to pray to and honor. And he really meant every nation—not just the Mediterranean or European countries. Similarly, he wanted holiness to be open to every member of the people of God. A sign of that was the increased number of laypeople and couples he held up as models of sanctity.

The basic idea, then, is that blesseds and saints blaze the trails that the Church follows. They create the history of the Church down through the centuries, and they are also the Church's spiritual memory. So they play a decisively important role in the life of the Church. They are witnesses to her vitality, and they confirm that her work of spreading the Gospel is on the right track.

In a nutshell, if the Church is able to educate saints, she herself is holy—thanks, of course, to the holiness of Christ.

This brings us back to what Mother Teresa often said: In the end, holiness is simply doing God's will in your daily life.

That's why John Paul II might—at least I like to think so—have regretted that he didn't live to see the canonization of two friends of his who lived out Mother Teresa's definition of holiness by fulfilling God's will in their daily lives. One was Jan Tyranowski, the catechist tailor, who introduced Wojtyla to the Carmelite mysticism of Saint John of the Cross and Saint Teresa of Avila. The other friend was Jerzy Ciesielski, one of the young people who came out of the Srodowisko group. He became an engineer and died in a tragic shipwreck on the Nile.

Now, it was Jan who always used to tell the young Karol something he, Jan, had once heard from a priest: "It's not hard to be a saint." His point was that the door of holiness is wide open to everyone.

26.

And the Wall Came Tumbling Down

This brings us to the "annus mirabilis" (year of miracles): 1989.

John Paul II wasn't expecting it. Yes, he did think that the system was doomed to collapse sooner or later because it was so socially unjust and economically inefficient. But the Soviet Union was still a geopolitical, military, and nuclear power. And so he didn't expect communism to fall so soon, though he always jokingly added that he was no prophet. And the last thing he expected was that freedom would come so swiftly and with so little bloodshed.

The way the revolution unfolded was indeed the most surprising thing about it. Apart from events in Romania—which had to do with infighting among Communist groups—the revolution was a peaceful movement that broke out simultaneously in pretty much all the capitals of the Soviet bloc: Berlin, Budapest, Warsaw, Prague, Sofia, Bucharest, and even, to a certain degree, Moscow.

The easy explanation that some proposed at the time—that the "new" Kremlin under Gorbachev (whose other merits I'm not denying) was steering the revolution toward nonviolent, peaceful transition—would thus seem unlikely. In reality, the pressure that toppled the system came from the people, who were moved by an irrepressible thirst for freedom and a total disillusionment with those who had promised to build a paradise on Earth.

The Holy Father regarded it as one of the greatest revolutions in history. In fact, reading it with the eyes of faith, he hailed it as a divine intervention, as a grace. He had no doubt that the fall of communism and the liberation of so many nations from the yoke of Marxist totalitarianism had to do with the revelations of Fatima and with the consecration of the world—especially Russia—to Our Lady, which she herself asked the Church and the Pope to perform. In the second Secret, she said: "If my requests are heeded, Russia will be converted and there will be peace; if not, she will spread her errors throughout the world. . . ."

And so on March 25, 1984, in Saint Peter's Square, John Paul II, spiritually united with all the world's bishops, made the act of consecration to Mary before a statue of Our Lady that had been brought from Fatima for that purpose. He didn't name Russia explicitly, but he alluded clearly to the nations that "particularly need to be thus entrusted and consecrated."

The Pope carried out Our Lady's wish. And at around the same time, the first signs that the Communist world was beginning to crumble started to appear.

That's not just my opinion, either, but the opinion of a lot of bishops from Eastern Europe.

You have to know how to read the signs of the times.

✦ ✦ ✦

It's true, of course, that communism collapsed because its political-ideological agenda, its social system, and, most of all, its economic plans had all failed. But it's equally true that there was another, prior failure, one Karol Wojtyla wrote about in his Encyclical Centesimus Annus: Communism was a spiritual failure because of its Promethean attempt to build a new world, one from which God would be banished, and to create a new man, whose conscience had no room for God.

The first ringing confirmation was delivered less than a month after the fall of the Berlin Wall. For the first time in the entire seventy years following the October Revolution, a president of the Supreme Council of the Communist Party, President Mikhail Gorbachev, visited the Vatican. He didn't march in at the head of the Cossack legions that were supposed to water their horses in the fountains of Saint Peter's Square, but came as the representative of a defeated ideology. History has an ironic sense of humor.

It was the end of the dramatic conflict between the world's supreme religious institution and the biggest attempt in human history to establish the atheistic creed by force.

This is more or less what the Pope and Gorbachev said as they exchanged their first long handshake:

John Paul II (in Russian): "Welcome. I'm very pleased to meet you."

Gorbachev: "But we've already been in touch more than once" (a reference to the letters he had exchanged with the Pope).

John Paul II: "Maybe on paper, but we still haven't had a chance to talk" (not finding the right words, he said this in Italian and the interpreter translated it into Russian).

At this point, they entered the Pope's private library and sat on opposite sides of the Pope's desk.

John Paul II: "Mr. President, I have prepared for this meeting with prayer."

The Pope related Gorbachev's response a few weeks later to some journalists on board an airplane. "My interlocutor was very happy that the Pope had prayed. He said that prayer is a sign of order, of spiritual values, and that we have such need of those."

That's exactly why it was a historic meeting, a historic sign of change. And Gorbachev didn't just insist on the importance of the spiritual dimension of the human person and its positive influence on civil life. He also showed a particular interest in the papal documents on the Church's social teaching.

Gorbachev talked about the situation in his country and stressed with real conviction that the Soviet Union could no longer keep going on as before. My impression, though, was that, at that point at least, Gorbachev wasn't thinking of the sort of deep or radical changes that would shortly occur in the USSR. He was thinking of the sorts of formal changes regarding transparency and freedom that were already part of perestroika. In other words, his intention was to create a communism with a human face, not to change Marxism from the inside.

The very fact that the leader of the Soviet Union was visiting the Vatican was already significant. What he said was equally significant: "Everything that has happened these last years in Eastern Europe could never have happened without the presence of this Pope, without the major role, including the major political role, that he has played on the world stage."

+   +   +

He was explicitly acknowledging what John Paul II had done. But, though he may not have realized or wanted to admit it, he was also acknowledging that by their sufferings, their martyrdom, and their resistance to state-imposed atheism, the churches—not just the Catholic Church—had nourished in millions of men and women the hope of one day regaining their freedom.

The Pope wanted to participate symbolically in the "pilgrimage" that entire peoples were now making toward freedom. He began with a trip to Czechoslovakia, the Communist country that had probably been most closed to the Christian message and most hostile to John Paul II.

In his welcome address to the Holy Father, President Vaclav Havel couldn't have expressed any better the historical eloquence of the papal visit. He called it a "miracle." Six months earlier, Havel had been arrested and imprisoned as an enemy of the state. Now, however, he was welcoming the first Slavic Pope, the first Pope to set foot in that land.

You could say that the "miracle" had already begun on November 12, 1989, when the Pope canonized Agnes of Bohemia. At least ten thousand Czechs, both from Czechoslovakia and abroad, turned up for the event. They discovered that they were united, strong, and no longer afraid.

The Pope said to them, "Your pilgrimage mustn't end today. It must continue." And the pilgrimage did continue. It continued to the threshold of Velvet Revolution, the ten days that changed Czech and Slovak history. It was almost like a second Prague Spring.

❖   ❖   ❖

The diktat of Yalta had been canceled, and Europe was no longer divided in two. The Iron Curtain had come down. The Cold War was over, as well. Meanwhile, though, the vast damage done by decades of Marxism was starting to come to light.

Communism had caused a real "anthropological disaster," as some said at the time. Man had emerged from the long winter of totalitarianism, but he seemed unable to realize that he was finally free. And while the legacy of communism continued to burden the East, the West was projecting a secularized model of society corrupted by consumerism and, at a deeper level, by a practical materialism that no longer valued life or perceived the worth of man himself.

When he returned to Poland in June 1991, John Paul II finally got a chance to bless the transition from totalitarianism to democracy. At the same time, though, he experienced how difficult it was for those long deprived of their freedom to make good use of it once they had gotten it back. Moreover, as his successor in Kraków, Cardinal Franciszek Macharski, pointed out, the Church, too, would have to learn to carry out its mission in a new situation, where daily confrontation with a dictatorial regime had given way to freedom and cultural-political pluralism.

The Pope chose the Decalogue and the commandment of love as the theme of his homilies. In other words, he wanted to emphasize that spiritual renewal is the indispensable foundation of every change or action in society. The moral dimension, he was saying, is the foundation of any democracy worthy of the name. When the trip was over, he confided to me the following assessment: "Not everyone welcomed the message, though."

But the Pope was most pained when the ex-Communists won the elections two years later. After having regained their freedom, the people—democratically—voted the Marxist Left into power. And the reason for the vote was not an endorsement of Marxism, but a critical attitude toward the capitalist regime and the free market. A lot of people weren't ready for the new system and now they were suffering because of the changes, because they were being asked to make huge sacrifices. And so people, especially the simpler ones, started saying that things had been better before.

We can say that more or less all of the ex-Communist countries were going through difficult times, and that the difficulty was inevitable. After all, it was a period of transition and adjustment. But it was also a precious opportunity: to change the course of history, to alter the relations among nations, and to close once and for all the terrible chapter written by two totalitarianisms that took turns trying to suffocate Europe's freedom and its Christian spirit.

So there couldn't have been a more symbolic scene than the joint appearance of John Paul II and Chancellor Kohl on June 23, 1996, at the Brandenburg Gate in Berlin. This gate, the Pope recalled, had been "occupied by two German dictatorships"—the Nazi and the Communist—and had even been turned into a wall by the latter. But now it was a "testimony to the fact that men had freed themselves by breaking the yoke of their oppression."

That was a very moving, very passionate moment for the Holy Father. But he also realized, with a certain bitterness I have to say, that a lot of Europeans hadn't understood the importance of the fact that a Pope—not because it was Wojtyla, but because it was the Pope—had walked through the gate that was supposed to immortalize the triumph of Hitler. And that he had beatified victims of the concentration camps in the very stadium where Hitler had watched the 1936 Olympics.

This is the point: John Paul II's walk through the Brandenburg Gate marked in his mind the definitive end of World War II. And the beatification ceremony in the stadium was the visible seal of God's victory in the tremendous battle against evil.

27.

No to Communism,
Not Yes to Capitalism

Barely six months after the fall of the Berlin Wall, the Pope was in Mexico. In an address to businessmen, he spoke about the changes in Eastern Europe. He said that "real socialism" might have been defeated, but that this did not automatically imply the triumph of the capitalistic system. The world was still full of the same poverty as before, of the same glaring inequalities in the distribution of resources. Which, the Pope said, were also due to the effects of a certain kind of unrestrained liberalism that lacked any concern for the common good, especially in the Third World.

It was a brave but responsible analysis that reflected the still-fluid nature of the moment. And yet, some Western commentators called the Pope's speech "scandalous." Some even went so far as to accuse John Paul II of a certain nostalgia for communism.

They didn't get it. More likely, they didn't want to get it. The Holy Father read history theologically and morally, not politically or economically. Now, from that particular vantage point he could see that, while Marxism had failed, we couldn't build a new social order solely on the basis of a system that regarded man as an instrument or a mere cog in the machine of production.

The most urgent task, then, was to retrieve the subjectivity of human work. Only then would it be possible to conceive of a model of economic development based on solidarity and participation. Because until the workers had become involved in decision making and in the redistribution of the means of production, no society would ever know peace and no country would ever know true progress.

The fact is, though, that in the first ten years of his pontificate, John Paul II had been regarded as a visceral anti-Communist, whereas now he was being presented as an anticapitalist, even a pro-Communist. And this might explain the longevity of a certain demagogic, or at least erroneous, interpretation of his social teaching in particular and of his humanism in general.

Thanks in part to his experience in Poland and his work as a philosopher, Karol Wojtyla had brought into his teaching as Pope a conception of man and history that wasn't indebted to any cultural or political system. In fact, he acknowledged the positive aspects both of Marxism and of capitalism, but he also spoke clearly about their defects. Setting aside the differences regarding the means of production—collectivized in one case, privately owned in the other—both systems actually shared the same flaw: They left no room for the centrality of man in economic and political processes.

In a word, Karol Wojtyla wasn't a party man. Or, to put it

bluntly, he was a man who didn't belong either to Moscow or to Washington. He was a man of God who was always open to everyone. He was a free man. And he never let himself be governed by political choices.

You've identified the necessary starting point for a deeper understanding of the "political" profile of the pontificate. What made it "political," of course, was how John Paul II interpreted and updated the Church's social teaching and how he used moral categories to describe socioeconomic phenomena.

That's how the Holy Father managed—especially in the encyclical *Centesimus Annus*—to sketch a social ideal that successfully combines justice and solidarity, the rights and duties of persons, ethics and sociopolitical involvement.

He did all this, though, without ever entering into policy decisions, or trying to determine how things should be done concretely. Otherwise, the Church would have abandoned its native territory. The Church has to stick to its pastoral mission and to critical reflection on whether or not social processes accord with the Creator's ways.

It was no idle phrase Karol Wojtyla used when he said that the Church shouldn't let any ideology or political school rob it of the "banner of justice." Justice is both one of the first requirements laid down by the Gospel and it is the core of the Church's social teaching.

The topic of justice leads logically to the topic of rights—the rights belonging to every human being, whose freedom and dignity must be defended, and the rights belonging to every people who, as a nation, can legitimately demand respect for their sov-

ereignty and independence, while at the same time taking part in the circle of solidarity with all other peoples making up the world community.

Here John Paul II reappropriated, as something "naturally Christian," the humanitarian principles that for a long time were the exclusive preserve of the Enlightenment and the French Revolution. By reintegrating human rights into Christian teaching, the Pope set them on a coherent ethical foundation, which is both the source and the guarantee of their indivisibility and universality.

So the Pope had absolutely no interest in re-creating the old distance between the Church and the world. On the contrary, he wanted to serve man and support his fundamental rights, starting with the right to life.

Now that we are on the topic, we have to say something about what may have been one of the least understood, but was surely one of the most controverted and criticized, aspects of John Paul II's pontificate. I mean his conception of the Church as a social force. To put it another way, the Pope thought that by working within society to serve the common good, the Church could make an important contribution to social renewal, though of course only as a consequence of its mission of incarnating the Gospel. In other words, the Church's aim was to bear witness to Christ, not to conquer or subjugate society, or to erase the distinction the Second Vatican Council made once and for all between the role of the Church and the role of the state.

Let me point out that pretty much all systems, and not just the totalitarian ones, have always tried to marginalize religion, or at least to drive it into the sacristy, or to exploit it for political purposes. Let me also point out that for a long time the arena of the public square belonged exclusively to the Left, even to the Communists, and I don't mean only in the Soviet Empire. Plus, some of Jesus' characteristic words, Christian words like *peace,* had become the absolute property of certain movements or parties.

Well, John Paul II refused to go along with all this. He said, "No!" And he went into the streets, into the public squares, because he didn't want to cede these spaces to others.

The Church is where man is. It tries to walk with man and society, but always on the road of moral engagement. It must never get directly involved in politics! That said, it's perfectly legitimate, a duty in fact, for the Church to make moral judgments, including moral judgments about society and politics—though the lay faithful are the ones who have to get involved in public life, especially in politics.

This reminds me of a major address by John Paul II that, unfortunately, never received the attention it deserved. I'm thinking of his October 1988 speech before the European Parliament in Strasbourg. In this speech, he dealt the deathblow to any temptation to return to the old religious integralism. And he also acknowledged that Christians, too, were guilty of their fair share of unauthorized "border crossings" between the realm of God and the realm of Caesar.

But there is one passage that especially deserves to be called to people's attention. For it helps us better grasp Wojtyla's understanding of secularity, and thus of the kind of distinction he thought should exist between the temporal and the spiritual. Similarly, it helps us better realize the extent to which John Paul II swept the old model of the intransigent Church into oblivion

and replaced it with the model of a Church able to deal with—
and that also means accept—the challenges of modern, plural-
istic society:

"Let me just say a word about Medieval Latin Christendom.
On the one hand, its recovery of the great Aristotelian tradition
did enable it to retrieve the conception of the state as a thing of
nature. On the other hand, it never escaped the integralist temptation of excluding from the temporal community those who did
not profess the true faith. By failing to distinguish between the
sphere of faith and the sphere of civil life, religious integralism,
which is still practiced today in another form, seems to be incompatible with the specific spirit of Europe as that spirit has
been shaped by the Christian message."

28.

The Global South

There was a natural and immediate rapport between John Paul II and the peoples of the Third World, who found in him an authoritative spokesman on the world stage, an "ally," as he called himself. But the rapport was spontaneous for another reason, as well: They both came from similar backgrounds of popular piety, poverty, and lack of freedom. Just as the Pope came from a country dominated by an authoritarian regime, the peoples of the Third World lived under the oppression of local dictators and the major powers that backed them.

The Holy Father had a very palpable experience of this at once personal and historical connection when he visited Angola in 1992. At the time, the country was still under a Marxist-style dictatorship. Speaking to the bishops at the end of the visit, the Pope drew a parallel between the Pentecost that they'd recently celebrated in Angola and the Pentecost the Pope celebrated at Gniezno when he first returned to what at the time was still Communist Poland. "The same process is at work," he said. "The geography is different, but it's the same system and the same program of ideological atheism. On the other side is the Church, which does not peddle some program, but which follows the Word of God and the promises of Christ."

For some time, especially since Vatican II, Catholicism had been shedding its somewhat too European and Western "garb." Ever since Pius XII, the Roman Curia had been undergoing a similar process of universalization. And John Paul II further accelerated this process. He was the first Pope to put a representative of black Africa, Cardinal Bernardin Gantin, at the head of one of the most important Vatican congregations, the Congregation of Bishops, which oversees the erection of dioceses and the appointment of bishops.

The Holy Father wanted the Curia to be in every respect an authentic, transparent expression of the universality of Catholicism. He knew, of course, that there were very qualified people, people of high caliber, in Italy, and he recognized that Italy deserved a lot of credit for its constant fidelity to Christ and to the papacy. Nevertheless, he wanted the Holy See truly to be the seat of the whole Church, and not just of one country.

This is why he called important people from every continent to the Vatican, where they would serve both as his collaborators in governing the Church and as representatives of their own local churches in the center of the Catholic world. You could say that by doing that the Pope achieved a true visible manifestation of episcopal collegiality.

There are a lot of examples to mention, but I'm thinking right now of people like Cardinal Francis Arinze from Nigeria or Cardinal Roger Etchegaray of France, who was the Pope's "envoy of peace" and whom he sent on any number of difficult missions in countries torn by war or emerging from disastrous conflict, from Lebanon to Bosnia-Herzegovina, and from Iraq to Sudan.

It was the encyclical Redemptoris Missio *(1991), though, that decisively shifted the Church's center of gravity toward the global. By means of the papal journeys, Pope John Paul II followed the shifting focus of evangelization from the global North (the First World) to the global South (the Third World). The trips gave him an opportunity to experience the tragedy of the Third World firsthand. They brought him into personal contact with the exploitation of Third World countries at the hands of rich nations and the conditions of poverty and social, cultural, and economic underdevelopment in which they were forced to live.*

It might sound banal and obvious to say that John Paul II never identified with the rich and powerful. But I will say it anyway in the hope that it conveys the extent to which his heart and soul, his concern as a man of God, were always focused on the weakest and most marginalized people of the world.

As he was planning his first trip to Africa in 1980, the Pope wanted to visit the poorest regions of the continent. He wanted to go to the Sahel, which was being devastated by the advance of the desert. He stopped for just a few hours in Upper Volta— today Burkina Faso—but that was enough for him to see with his own eyes the tragedy of a "country ravaged by drought." Ouagadougou, the capital, was covered by a red blanket of sand. The faucets were completely dry. There were carcasses of animals in the streets. And everywhere you saw signs of a terrible famine.

All of this made such a deep impression on the Holy Father that, very shortly after his arrival, he asked four African experts— Cardinals Gantin, Thiandoum, and Zoungrana, and Archbishop

Sangaré—to help him draft a statement. They found a table, sat
down, and worked out the famous appeal that the Pope read
soon after that: "I, John Paul II, Bishop of Rome and Successor
of Peter, am here as the voice of the voiceless; the voice of the
innocent who have died for lack of water and bread; the voice of
the mothers and fathers who have watched their children die
without understanding why."

*Thanks to the trips, thanks to his very presence, the Pope was
able publicly to support, and speak on behalf of, the right of
Third World peoples to more justice and freedom.*

His 1983 trip to Central America included a stop in Haiti, which
at the time was under the thumb of the powerful Duvalier family. As he was reading his speech, the Pope came to the part
where he quoted the slogan of a local eucharistic congress:
"Something has to change." At that point, the Holy Father noticed how his huge, enthusiastic audience was reacting to those
words. So he began repeating the slogan more and more vigorously.

    Following that, people began turning out in huge numbers.
Jean-Claude Duvalier was extremely nervous, and he asked the
Pope to tone down his farewell speech. But the Pope replied that
he couldn't do that in good conscience. "Because it's true," he
said, "something has to change here! The people are suffering
here. Things can't go on like this!" The experts in political science
tell us that this was the first step on Haiti's road to democracy.

*The encounter with the Third World contributed a lot to the
Pope's and the Church's thinking about what had become the
global scale of the "social question," and about the correspond-*

ing need to lay down new principles to govern the relations among peoples. After all, the world was becoming ever more globalized and interdependent, but for that very reason there was an increasing risk that poverty and injustice would spread.

The result of this reflection was the encyclical Sollicitudo Rei Socialis. The encyclical denounced the failure of Third World development projects and the growing gap between an ever richer First World and an ever poorer Third World. The Pope then went on to call the world's peoples to renew their cooperation in a spirit of real reciprocity and solidarity. He condemned not only the ideologies and the various forms of imperialism but also what he considered to be the newer, more sophisticated forms of neocolonialism, which presented a facade of liberality while continuing to manipulate the choices of individuals and peoples.

In this context, Sollicitudo was the first papal document that addressed the "structures of sin."

The phrase doesn't apply to any one country in particular, but the Holy Father definitely had a special concern for Latin America. He saw it as the continent of hope, both for the Church and for humanity. And yet it was precisely in Latin America that he observed structures that not only went against human dignity but that generated more and more poverty. He was anguished when he looked around and saw things like widespread illiteracy, miserable *favelas* (shantytowns), massive unemployment, the breakup of families, and, on top of that, a tendency to seek escape from these horrors in the empty promises of fundamentalist sects.

The option for the poor was always a firm priority in the Pope's apostolic ministry. That's why he never condemned the liberation movements—the authentic ones. What he did condemn were the movements that led to a new slavery—to Marxism—because they used the masses as a vehicle to achieve power.

He tried to understand the problems of suffering people, because he wanted these people to perceive his love for them. And to realize that, even if the Church can't solve their problems, it can at least give them hope, which is already a big help in such situations.

One of the merits of Sollicitudo Rei Socialis, then, was that it broke not only the (more recent, and yet more dangerous) identification of Christianity with liberalism but also the (more ancient, and yet more deeply rooted) identification of Christianity with Western civilization. This laid an important foundation for rethinking the Church's mission in the East. Or, as Pope John Paul II would say, for making the third millennium the millennium of the evangelization of the Asian continent.

Eighty-five percent of all non-Christians live in Asia. Think of a gigantic country like China, which is still basically closed. Or of the traditional religions. Or of the more than thirty Muslim countries that impose more or less tough restrictions on preaching the Gospel. And yet, despite past mistakes, there would seem to be room in Asia for a religion like Christianity, which combines contemplation of God with concern for man and his problems.

I think I can say that one of the things that pained John Paul II most was the failure to understand his attitude toward China and the Chinese.

The Pope wished China well. He cordially felt a true and deep friendship toward the Chinese people. So much so that he even started learning a bit of the language. It wasn't because he was planning a trip, which he knew was next to impossible at the time. If nothing else, he wanted to be able to greet the Chinese people directly in his Christmas and Easter radio messages. So he wanted to give a sign to the Catholic faithful—who are among the truest of the true—and to tell them that the Pope was with them. But he also wanted to give a sign to the entire Chinese people, to make them understand that he wished them well.

The Holy Father always tried to keep up good relations with the Chinese. He respected their pride in their identity, and he wanted to help China find its due place in the international community. This was also the attitude of the Catholic Church. The Church looked forward to helping China in this way as part of its contribution as a religious and spiritual body to fostering the human family and promoting world peace.

So the point was never interference in China's internal affairs. Absolutely not. On the contrary, it was to support China in shouldering the major role that it is called to play in the family of nations.

That was John Paul II's wish. And I can assure you that it conveyed his spirit, as well. Unfortunately, he was met with misunderstanding, and that pained him greatly. Now that he is gone, we have to keep hoping that China will find the way to respond to his wish.

29.

A New Adversary

The great film director Wim Wenders has a talent for depicting both reality and its counterfeits. He showed the same talent in describing the "worm" that has burrowed into the heart of contemporary man. "I believe," he said, "that religion begins with an act of humility: the act of not thinking you're the Creator." His point was that man today suffers under the temptation, or at least the illusion, of being able to decide by himself alone what is good and what is evil, without taking any account of God and His truth.

Wenders's remark was indeed an exact picture of the increasing secularization of Western society (the world's chief representative of liberal ideology) and of the consequent progressive loss of the West's Christian character. By the same token, the disappearance of yesterday's Great Enemy, Marxism's systematic institutionalization of atheism, left the Church facing an even more insidious threat: an everyday, practical materialism that was producing more and more people who "live as if God didn't exist," in the words of John Paul II.

✦   ✦   ✦

This was the great challenge that the Holy Father found himself facing once the conflict with communism was over. There was an increasingly blatant indifference to religion, originating from a loss of a sense of transcendence. At the same time, faith was being visibly reduced to the merely subjective. There's another issue that you have to remember as well: the pollution riding in on the tide of consumerism that at the time was flooding Eastern Europe from the West.

In response, Pope John Paul II wrote the encyclical Veritatis Splendor *to highlight the danger posed by a certain dominant culture of moral relativism, whose tendency to bracket the imperatives of the moral law threatened to undermine the very foundations of democratic society. The Pope was also concerned about potentially serious fallout in other areas as well, such as in bioscience, where research was already encroaching on the sacredness of life.*

The appearance of the encyclical provoked furious reactions, fierce criticisms, and endless polemics. Some suggested that the Church was turning back the clock to Pope Pius IX's Syllabus of Errors.

At times, it seemed as if the Pope were the only one left defending the principles of morality. But he was perfectly capable of distinguishing between the opinion of the media and the opinion of normal folks, including non-Catholics. And that was part of the genius of Karol Wojtyla: He never let the press dictate his movements. He never gave in to pessimism, either. He would always say, "Christ is in the Church." In other words, there would be calm after the storm. There would be a springtime after the winter.

The Magisterium was obliged to take part in another, even harder and more wearying, battle in defense of human life from conception to natural death. The result was the encyclical Evangelium Vitae. Once more, the Pope seemed to be a lonely voice crying in the wilderness of egoism and conformism. He looked like the last bulwark against the "culture of death" that blithely continued condoning legal abortion. He seemed especially alone after the parliaments of a number of countries had arrogated for themselves the right to define the boundary between life and death.

At the time, abortion was king. The situation had gotten so bad that people were pushing it as if it were an actual right. The preparatory document for the Cairo Conference on Population and Development explicitly called for a demographic policy that would use abortion as a general method of birth control. And this was the proposal of a United Nations committee!

You're right that at first John Paul II seemed to be alone in the fight. But as time went on more and more people around the world—most of them laity—dedicated themselves to the mission of defending life. New movements in favor of life sprang up all over the place. The John Paul II Institute for Studies on Marriage and the Family was founded in Rome, and a number of campuses were set up in different countries. And that was a good thing, too, because in the meantime another battle was flaring up over the family.

✦   ✦   ✦

Thick clouds of individualism had already hung over Western culture and society for some time, and they boded no good. But in 1994—the Year of the Family, ironically—there was an all-out assault on the family. It called into question the family's nature and stability, contested its role as the fundamental cell of society, and even challenged the very meaning of love between spouses. Leading the charge was the UN, in the pages of the same Cairo document you mentioned just now.

Pope John Paul II had this to say in his "Letter to Families": "The family is placed at the center of the great struggle between good and evil, between life and death, between love and all that is opposed to love." He sent an even more strongly worded letter to the world's heads of states and to the secretary-general of the UN. The Pope was pursuing a vigorous, impassioned strategy in the grand style—but not a crusade. It wasn't merely a defensive action, either. It was the positive proposal of a model of the family that was both suited to the times and in harmony with God's plan.

I remember one Sunday in a parish in Rome. The Holy Father unexpectedly departed from the written text of his speech. It was as if his heart were venting its pent-up frustration: "We've got to be bold and unyielding!" He tried to moderate his tone a bit, observing that the Pope is a naturally "gentle man"—those were his exact words. In the end, though, he couldn't restrain himself: "But his principles have to be rigorous."

The point is that, for him, the family was fundamentally important. He was convinced that the future of the Church, of society, and of the peoples of the world depended on the family. And it pained him to see international organizations phasing the word *family* out of their documents and replacing it with other highly ambiguous and generic terms.

On top of that, the debate gradually expanded from abortion to include new hot topics like cohabitation, euthanasia, homosexuality, and certain "advances" of medical science. Then there was a whole "debate about man," which seemed about to lead to a radical redefinition of ethical norms and even of the very thing we call "the human being."

You can't change the nature of man and woman, though! It's one thing to rethink certain rigid boundaries that still exist between men and women because of biology or the body, and it's another thing to distort the fact that "male and female he created them." If we disrespect the laws of nature, we jeopardize the future of the human race. We'll have to pay a heavy price tomorrow for the damage we do today.

It was over this precise issue that John Paul II had to do battle with the contemporary world, or at least with a certain side of it. What was the Pope supposed to do—bless human weakness? All he did was show the right path, the path of harmony with God's creative design. In other words, he tried to follow the Lord, as he always did. He was the shepherd entrusted with the guidance of his people. But people didn't—or didn't want to— understand him.

Now, everything we've been talking about clearly signaled a revival of Enlightenment rationalist culture, a revival whose political consequences soon made themselves felt. Couldn't we say that this revival was the ultimate reason behind the refusal of the Pope's request to insert an explicit mention of the Christian roots of Europe in the new European Constitution?

Some commentators have written that the European Parliament's refusal greatly pained the Pope. The issue that concerned him there, though, wasn't his own opinions, but the foundations of Europe. Yes, the Holy Father was grieved, but it was because he saw that Europe couldn't acknowledge what it actually needs most today: a recovery of the values that built it and made it great in the world.

Probably at no other time during his pontificate was John Paul II so attacked, criticized, and even insulted as during the long, tough battle over morality which we've recounted here. Yet he never wavered. He defended life and he reasserted the truth of God, though he also spoke out in the name of the truth of man and of freedom of conscience. He challenged the culture of relativism, even as his encyclical Fides et Ratio *opened up an unprecedented chapter in the Church's dialogue with reason, and, in a sense, with modernity.*

And so, contrary to the spin some have put on it, the Pope's battle on this front had nothing to do with a reactionary campaign in a spirit of intransigence and closure. John Paul II was proposing a humanism, a humanism he thought could help contemporary man rediscover the authentically moral meaning of his history and destiny.

30.

The Spirit of Assisi

A certain highly regarded intellectual once famously said that in 1989 man had reached the "end of history." By that he meant that, after 1989, the international situation was sufficiently stable to banish fears of any recurrence of the terrible tragedies of the past. This was only a hypothesis, of course, but behind it was the belief that two world wars, Hiroshima, and some close shaves with nuclear holocaust had finally taught mankind its "lesson."

Thus, when the Gulf War broke out in 1990, a lot of people took it as a mere "traffic accident." There was another reason for this reaction: In spite of giving off a strong whiff of petrodollars, the war could in some respects be considered a just one. After all, so the argument went, a small country (Kuwait) had been invaded and occupied by a stronger bully of a neighbor (Iraq). So something had to be done to stanch the wound.

As soon as the Gulf crisis broke out in August, John Paul II began doing everything in his power to avoid a conflict. He argued that in our day war could no longer be regarded as a just or effective tool for resolving international disputes. He also pointed out that in cases like Vietnam, Lebanon, and Afghanistan, war not only didn't resolve the problems but made them much worse by unleashing the devastating power of contemporary weapons technology.

And then, with respect to the specific issue of Iraq, the "justice" of the war aims seemed dubious. The goal was to rectify a violation of international law, but the refusal to explore all available diplomatic avenues of dialogue, mediation, and negotiation itself amounted to another betrayal of the same international law. And as late as the general audience of January 16, the Pope, joined by thousands of the faithful, was still pleading with the world: "No more war; war is a journey of no return."

But the war machine was incapable of stopping. There were too many interests at stake. The president of the United States did not alert the Pope. It was a journalist who rang up Archbishop Jean-Louis Tauran (today a cardinal, at the time the Vatican equivalent of a foreign minister) to notify him that they were bombarding Baghdad. And to think that at seven o'clock the evening before, Tauran had received the American ambassador without hearing a single word about the invasion. But perhaps the ambassador himself was in the dark. Or maybe the American government was unhappy with this Pope who talked "too much" about peace.

It's true. Some people were shocked that John Paul II would speak so insistently about peace at a time like that. Some thought he was "neutral," or embraced "moral equivalence," or was even a pro-Arab, Third World radical. On the other hand, though, there were others who tried to enlist him in the ranks of the pacifists—in other words, to slap him with an ideological or political label.

If I may say so, this was a genuine insult to a fundamentally meek, peace-loving man who followed the way of nonviolence, as we would say today. The insult was even worse considering his background as a Pole who had personally experienced two totalitarianisms. Most of all, though, it was a slap in the face for a Pope who was a witness to the God of peace and the spokesman of humanity's yearning for peace.

On the morning of January 17, after having found out what was happening, the Pope celebrated the Mass for peace in his private chapel. He was saddened—profoundly so, in fact. It was unconceivable to him that no means could be found to stop the conflict.

"I have done all that was humanly possible," he said at one of the general audiences. But he didn't stop with recriminations over what hadn't been done. He immediately called together his collaborators from the Secretariat of State in order to decide what steps to take on the humanitarian and diplomatic level. The result was a first major initiative: a summit meeting in Rome among representatives of the episcopates of the countries involved either directly or indirectly in the Gulf War.

Well, the Holy Father had been right. He was right in judging that the war was a totally mistaken endeavor and futile from the beginning and, more important, that it presaged tragic suffering for the civil population. He was also right in predicting that the war would result in new and serious complications throughout the whole Middle East.

◆   ◆   ◆

The Gulf War might have seemed like a distant incident on the periphery, a situation that would have no significant impact on the general climate of stability. But the war that broke out almost simultaneously in the former Yugoslavia and dragged on for years like a spreading cancer dispelled any illusion that the world had set out on the road to peace. Most of all, the war shook up Europeans, who were shocked to hear the rumble of cannons on their own soil again.

At the time, there were some who suggested a certain contradiction between the Holy Father's absolute opposition to the Gulf War and his insistence on the right to "humanitarian intervention" in the fierce ethnic conflict that was tearing apart Bosnia-Herzegovina. The fact of the matter is that the two situations were radically different. A war between two states is one thing. But intervention—intervention decided on by supranational authorities or institutions like the UN or the European Community to disarm an aggressor who threatens the very survival of a people—is something else.

The butchery in the Balkans finally ended. Only at that point did people begin to understand more fully what John Paul II meant when he wrote in the encyclical Centesimus Annus *that war could lead to a "suicide of humanity," with no winners or losers.*
    What was needed after the fall of the Berlin Wall was the creation of a new international order. The UN should have focused on putting out the many brushfires that threatened what was already a very fragile peace. But nothing was done. Meanwhile,

*the collapse of Soviet totalitarianism removed the constraints
that had suppressed a number of phenomena that now began to
explode onto the scene: nationalism, racism, violence, and even
conflict fueled by religious hatred, as in the case of the former
Yugoslavia.*

*John Paul II foresaw the new turmoil that was about to ap-
pear on the world scene. This was a stroke of Providence, as was
his realization that laying the foundations for a true peace would
require beginning with the basic pillar of religion. He believed
that the religions of the world needed to reclaim their decisive
role in promoting a culture of peace and in fostering the growth
of a genuine solidarity among peoples.*

Yes, the suggestion of a religious path to peace had a long history
behind it. It began with the Holy Father's journeys to places as
far-flung as Casablanca and India, which put him in contact
with other Christian churches and other religions. Meanwhile,
he was more and more convinced that the growing awareness of
the damage done by atheism and materialism created an opportunity for religion to return from its exile on the margins of society and start playing an important role again in social affairs.

At the same time, the Pope realized that the struggle for peace
was monopolized by certain movements and political forces that
transformed peace into an ideology and, for that very reason,
turned it into a cause of conflict and division. Ironically, this was
happening at a time when peace was threatened, international
relations were strained, and there was a certain escalation in the
arms race.

The Pope also treasured an old dream of Bonhoeffer's: a world
assembly of Christian churches that would forthrightly proclaim
"Christ's peace to a world insanely bent on self-destruction."

Bonhoeffer never lived to see his idea realized, since he died a hero at the hands of the Nazis. But fifty years later, the German physicist-philosopher Carl Friedrich von Weizsäcker suggested it again in his book *The Time Is Short*. And Weizsäcker repeated his suggestion in a conversation with the Pope.

In the background, then, was a kind of spiritual chain linking prophetic people from very different contexts.

John Paul II thoroughly studied the question from every angle. He found a most helpful collaborator in the Pontifical Council for Justice and Peace at the time under the presidency of Cardinal Etchegaray. Then, one day, it all crystallized in a brilliant inspiration. "I've realized what we need," the Holy Father confided to me, "a prayer for peace with all the religions!" He was also the one to choose Assisi, the city of Saint Francis, which he thought was the most suitable place from which to invite representatives of the world's religions to set out as pilgrims on the road to peace: an unprecedented event.

The result was the World Day of Prayer for Peace, which was held on October 27, 1986, in Assisi. For the first time ever, adherents of all the religions—representing more than four billion men and women—met at the same time in the same place in order to beg God for the gift of peace. On the Pope's right were Archbishop Methodios, the representative of the Ecumenical Patriarchate, Robert Runcie, the archbishop of Canterbury, and other Orthodox and Protestant leaders. On his left were the Dalai Lama and the other non-Christian delegates.

As if to enshrine the historic moment, there wasn't a single battlefield death anywhere in the world that day.

◆   ◆   ◆

After centuries of divisions, conflicts, and misunderstandings, the meeting at Assisi—actually, you'd have to say it was the event itself, more than what was said there—was a kind of watershed in the history of interreligious relations. Praying together in a universal language, the representatives of the different religions rediscovered their original nature and inspiration, though without compromising their respective spiritualities. By the same token, they discovered the communion that binds them together as brothers.

Assisi was probably John Paul II's boldest, most courageous, newest, and most constructive initiative. At the time, though, it was also the one that provoked the most hostility and controversy, however incredible that might seem to us today. And there's good reason to think that at least some of the criticisms emanated from the ranks of the Roman Curia itself. Consider the fact that in a 1987 conversation with Andrea Riccardi, the founder and head of the Community of Sant'Egidio, John Paul II said to him, though in a joking tone, "Let's keep going; let's continue, even though they almost excommunicated me."

Yes, it's true that there was a certain dissent, but, when you consider how novel the gathering at Assisi was, it was pretty limited. The harshest accusations came from the Lefebvrists. And there were critical judgments even in the Church and the Curia, but most of the critics were older people who were afraid that the day of prayer in Assisi might open the door to syncretism, to the idea of a big spiritual melting pot where every religion is as good as every other. But that completely missed the point. *Completely.* The Holy Father explained over and over again that we met together to pray, not that we met to pray together.

The Pope was happy that evening in Assisi. I remember his words: "That was a really extraordinary day. Representatives of all the religions gathered for the first time to ask God for peace. Plus, there was no fighting anywhere today. That was another great sign!" I also remember that many of the participants came to tell him how grateful they were. They said that without him, without his courage, the world's spiritual leaders would never have met in Assisi.

Once again, the Holy Father was right. He was a prophet who foresaw the future. And we—I mean the Church in general— haven't always managed to follow him.

That's why we have to thank Benedict XVI, who, unlike others, did understand John Paul II and always stood by him. And since I'm on the topic, I'd like to contradict the claims of those who said, and still say, that Cardinal Ratzinger didn't agree with the Pope regarding Assisi. That's completely false.

The meeting in Assisi also marked a new beginning. The "spirit of Assisi," which subsequently continued to spread, thanks to the efforts of the Community of Sant'Egidio, had an effect on the world's religions. It galvanized in them a renewed commitment to building peace and to repudiating every form of sectarianism or legitimation of violence. For Jews, Christians, and Muslims, this commitment translated into a pledge to work together to bring "justice and peace, pardon, life, and love" to the Earth.

The very fact of pledging this commitment with one accord before God and man was already a sign of hope. No matter what anyone says, it was a sign that will never be erased.

31.

The New Martyrs

I think that from the time when I went to live with Archbishop Karol Wojtyla—so from the time when I really got to know him—the year 2000 always played a role in his thoughts and hopes. It wasn't just for the obvious reason that 2000 would mark the beginning of a new millennium. Since the turn of the millennium would coincide with the two thousandth anniversary of Jesus' birth, he thought it should be an occasion for the moral and spiritual renewal of the Catholic community.

The then archbishop of Kraków spoke of the millennium as a "New Advent" in his 1976 Lenten meditations at the Vatican. Upon his election to the papacy, he said almost exactly the same thing in his first encyclical, Redemptor Hominis. This reference foreshadowed his decision to proclaim a Great Jubilee, which would involve not only Christians but, in some sense, all mankind. The Jubilee would call Catholics to an examination of conscience in preparation for a radical transformation of their lives. But it would have a strong ecumenical flavor, as well.

◆ ◆ ◆

That's right. The Holy Father intended the Jubilee as a provi-
dential chance for Christians to come to terms with the past and
to purify their memory of all the sins, mistakes, and forms of
counterwitness they'd been guilty of down through the centuries—like the Crusades, to take just one example.

By the same token, the Jubilee was supposed to strengthen dialogue with the other Christian churches and the other religions.
But the Pope's biggest concern was that we should request forgiveness without asking anything in return. The gratuity of the
gesture, he would say, was an indispensable condition of its credibility and efficacy.

*The fact is that John Paul II had already been walking down this
path for some time. The trips were a natural setting for the mea
culpas. For example, speaking in May 1995 to a crowd gathered
in the Czech city of Olomouc, he said, "Today I, the Pope of the
Church of Rome, ask forgiveness in the name of all Catholics for
all the wrongs done to non-Catholics." The Pope made the same
request, using more or less the same words, almost one hundred
times.*

*For this very reason, though, some churchmen, even some
cardinals, criticized the Pope's requests for forgiveness. Many of
the faithful, too, watched this development with a certain un-
ease. They were unsettled by the prospect—mistaken, to be sure,
but understandable from their point of view—that the history of
the Church might turn out to have been nothing but one long
string of sins.*

◆ ◆ ◆

Before starting down that path, I'm sure the Pope asked himself, What does the Gospel tell us? What would Jesus do in this circumstance? And then, seeing things in the light of faith, as a sign of divine Providence, he undoubtedly made the decision with a serene heart. That serenity is what enabled him to avoid becoming discouraged and to maintain a certain detachment in the face of subsequent opposition.

But there were also people who supported him. I have to mention Cardinal Etchegaray again as an example of such support. And then the resistance and doubt gradually began to disappear. The mea culpas turned out to be a key to opening the doors of ecumenical and interreligious dialogue.

And yet, up until that point, the Pope was the one taking the initiative. He was the only one making public declarations of repentance. Before that, not a single episcopate had critically reread the history of the Catholic Church in their country or made statements like the Pope's.

Things changed, though, on March, 12, 2000, when the Jubilee Day of Forgiveness was held at Saint Peter's. For the first time, the whole Church joined in imploring God to forgive the sins and omissions by which Christians had not only stained their own consciences but had also (in the words of Vatican II) "disfigured the face of the Church." It was the whole Church that solemnly pledged "never again" to betray the Gospel and the service of truth.

The Holy Father referred to the event later that day in his Angelus address. Afterward, as he came away from the window, I noticed that he was still deeply moved. It was one of the few times when he didn't make any comment. He said nothing about the part in the ceremony where he had spent several minutes embracing and kissing the feet of the corpus on the crucifix. He didn't speak of what he had felt at that moment.

But when I recall the look on his face, it was if he were saying, "It had to be done; it had to be done."

Another major Jubilee celebration took place on May 7 in the Colosseum: the commemoration of the twentieth-century witnesses of the faith. They included a few well-known, or even famous, names. But most of the witnesses belonged to an immense throng of martyrs who had remained anonymous, or who had even disappeared without a trace. "As it were, the unknown soldiers of God's great cause," was how the Pope put it.

These martyrs included priests and laypeople, especially catechists. They included Catholics, Orthodox, and Protestants. Together, they made up a martyrology that defied confessional divisions, political frontiers, and ideological barriers. There were new categories of martyrs, as well: not only martyrs for faith but also martyrs for things like justice, peace, and the defense of man. This was a further confirmation that the churches, and their faithful, had taken the side of the poor, the excluded, and the oppressed.

The Holy Father made a special point of insisting that the witnesses of faith should be as ecumenically representative as possible. He would often say that "the martyrs unite us. Their voice is much louder than the divisions of the past."

At this point, I'd like to highlight a particular aspect of the ceremony. The seventh category of martyrs consisted of Chris-

tians who gave their lives for love of Christ and the brethren in
the Americas. The concluding prayer mentioned several such
Christians, including Archbishop Oscar Romero of San Salvador,
who was gunned down while celebrating the Eucharist. Well, I
should say that it was the Holy Father himself who decided to
have Romero included. As the event drew nearer, there were
polemics and false conjectures. But the Pope put an abrupt end
to all that. When the organizers went to see him, he expressly
asked them to add the name—and these were his exact words—
of "that great witness of the Gospel."

They were also more or less the same words John Paul II used
in 1983 when he very firmly refused the suggestion of a few
Latin American bishops that he shouldn't visit Romero's tomb
because the slain archbishop was too politically controversial.
"No, the Pope has to go. Romero was a bishop who was gunned
down at the very heart of his ministry as a pastor, during the celebration of the Holy Mass."

*By the end of the second millennium, then, the Church had
once more become a Church of martyrs. Religious persecution
hadn't ended with the disappearance of atheist communism. It
had just shifted geographically. Now the epicenter was China
and the Islamic countries influenced by fundamentalists. But
pretty much everywhere, though in less brutal ways, religious
freedom was being attacked and violated with alarming frequency. Sometimes the assault was due to government interference; sometimes it stemmed from the tendency to expel religion
from public life and relegate it to the privacy of conscience.
Whatever the cause, there are reportedly 200 million persecuted
Christians and more than 400 million persons who suffer discrimination on account of their faith.*

✦   ✦   ✦

The Holy Father never forgot his pilgrimage to the Hill of Crosses near Šiauliai, Lithuania.

The first crosses were planted after the insurrection against the Russians in 1863. But the tradition continued, especially during the Soviet occupation. The Communists would bulldoze the hill, and the next day the Lithuanians would cover it with new crosses. It went on like that for years.

The Pope spent a long time walking through the jungle of crosses. There was even one commemorating the attempt on his life. He had a look of deep sadness in his eyes, and he kept murmuring, "The world should come here to see this sign of Lithuania's faith and martyrdom."

And yet, John Paul II knew how to read Lithuania's tragic history in the light of Providence. The Baltic countries had finally thrown off the yoke of foreign occupation. For the first time, he was free to visit territories that had once belonged to the Soviet Empire. Above all, though, the Hill of Crosses was a symbol of hope—of a hope that, sustained by faith in God and the courage of men, was sure of eventual victory.

And if something like this could happen in the past despite fierce persecution, then it could happen again in the future.

So the Jubilee was a lot of things. It was the incredible meeting between the Pope and two million young people at Tor Vergata. It was his pilgrimage down the paths of salvation history. Above all, though, it was an authentic spiritual revolution, because it tapped Vatican II's potential for renewal to give the world a fresh taste of the vitality and richness of the Christian people.

John Paul II gathered the fruit of the Jubilee celebrations and turned it into the guiding thread of an apostolic letter, Novo Millennio Ineunte, which presented a Church more focused on the Word of God and the proclamation of the Gospel, a Church that would be "the home and the school of communion." The letter also carried an invitation, made with all the Pope's missionary fire, to set aside laziness and fear and to live the Christian virtue of hope in our everyday lives. "We need to set sail," he wrote.

The Holy Father devoted the last three years of the millennium to reflection on the Trinity. By doing that, he put the Jubilee on a Trinitarian foundation, and so reaffirmed the picture of the Church that he had sketched in his first three encyclicals. Now he was unfolding the implications of that vision: a new program for the Church's life and mission centered on the mystery of God.

You see, that's exactly the kind of person Karol Wojtyla was. He never stopped to look back at what he'd already done. No, he was always looking ahead. The Jubilee had gone well, and we had to thank God for that, but we also had to think of the future and to forge new directions for pastoral work and mission.

Obviously, he couldn't be expected to be as physically robust, and perhaps as enthusiastic, as he had been twenty years earlier. But his vision—of history, of the Church, of his pontificate and his apostolic endeavors, and, above all, of the work of salvation that was happening in those years—that vision was the same from start to finish. He always defined his goals with the utmost clarity, even though the Curia or the local churches might not always pursue them in the way he wanted.

And yet, when the Jubilee was over, a lot of journalists started opining that the pontificate was also over, and that this Pope no

longer had any new surprises up his sleeve. Some even talked of
resignation (partly) on account of his advancing illness.

If those journalists were to review the period between 2001 and
2005, they would have to offer a nice mea culpa of their own.
The fact is that those were very full years. They were full of
drama and suffering because of events in the world—starting
with the attack on the Twin Towers—and in the Church—things
like the pedophilia scandal in the United States or the Archbishop Milingo affair. But they were also years full of new developments, such as numerous trips to places like the Near East,
the Balkans, Kraków (to consecrate the world to the Divine
Mercy), and even beyond the Urals. Then there were events like
the encyclical on the Eucharist, or certain breakthroughs in
evangelization and the dialogue with Orthodoxy.

As for the issue of resignation, I'd like to point out that John
Paul II actually dealt with the question even before the year
2000. Paul VI had decided to exclude cardinals who were over
eighty from papal elections. Similarly, John Paul II wondered
whether the Pope wasn't obliged to resign from office on reaching eighty, or, as he put it in his will, whether his eightieth birthday wouldn't mean the time had come "to say with Simeon of the
Bible, 'Nunc dimittis.' "

The Holy Father thus decided to consult with his closest collaborators, among them Cardinal Ratzinger, prefect of the Con-
gregtion for the Doctrine of the Faith. And, after reflecting and
examining the documents left by Paul VI on the subject, he
came to the conclusion that he should submit to God's will—
that is, that he should remain in office for as long as God was
pleased to keep him there. "God has called me. He will recall
me, too, according to his will."

At the same time, John Paul II did work out a procedure for resigning should he no longer be able to carry out his papal mission. You see, then, that he actually did give serious thought to the possibility of resignation. And yet, he decided to do God's will to the end. He accepted his Cross. He wanted to follow Christ's example and carry his burden to the end of his life.

32.

It Took Six Hands

John Paul II was pushing manfully, but he just couldn't seem to get the Holy Door to open. For onlookers at Saint Paul Outside the Walls who didn't know what was going on, there was a moment of embarrassment. Only a moment, though. Because it immediately became clear: It wasn't that the Pope couldn't open the door, but that he was waiting. He was waiting for the Orthodox Metropolitan Athanasios representative and the archbishop of Canterbury, George Carey, to lend a hand. With all six hands pushing, the door swung open. And then all three knelt in unison.

For the first time in history, the Bishop of Rome, the Successor of Peter, and the most senior representatives of Orthodoxy and Protestantism jointly opened a Holy Door and stepped side by side into the Basilica of the Apostle of the Gentiles, which as such is the ecumenical basilica par excellence.

The Pope himself took the initiative. He wanted there to be a deeply meaningful sign in the presence of representatives of the entire Christian world. After the ceremony, the participants had lunch together. They had been gathered around the altar; now they were gathered around the table. The atmosphere was remarkable. And in the name of all the participants, the Holy Father thanked God for the "great gift" of that day.

The scene we've just described, which took place on January 18, 2000, symbolized the whole trajectory of the ecumenical movement, with all its peaks and valleys. On the one hand, a lot of old difficulties had recently resurfaced to aggravate ancient controversies. On the other hand, Catholics, Orthodox, and Protestants still firmly wished to wipe away the painful legacy of the past and erase the "scandal" of Christian division that had continued on into the third millennium.

That's exactly why one of the first things John Paul II did after his election was to arrange a visit to the Ecumenical Patriarchate of Constantinople. He wanted to send a clear signal that the Catholic Church, and in particular the new Pope, firmly intended to carry forward the dialogue with all the Orthodox churches, and to resist discouragement over the inevitable obstacles.

I was present at a conversation where the Holy Father said, "Ecumenism is the will of Christ, *ut unum sint,* that they may all be one. It's the will of the Second Vatican Council. And it's my program, which I will follow in spite of the difficulties, the misunderstandings, and the occasional insults."

Karol Wojtyla became Pope at a time when ecumenism was stagnating. The initial postconciliar rush of enthusiasm over progress in the "dialogue of charity" and the revival of common prayer was now over. It had given way to a period of theological debate, which was much less spectacular—indeed, was actually more irksome and complex on account of the many issues needing to be cleared up. In spite of that, John Paul II worked to lessen the distance. His travels played a big part in that effort. Of course, as he himself had predicted, he also had to put up with the occasional insult.

He was the first Pope in history to visit the "kingdom" of the Reformation: Scandinavia. Church leaders didn't always receive him in an appropriate manner. Indeed, in Norway and Denmark, a few Lutheran bishops boycotted the prayer services that had been scheduled with the Pope.

In spite of that, the visit to Scandinavia yielded abundant fruit. For by presenting himself as a brother, a friend, and, most important, as a witness to Christ, John Paul II was able to break down much of the antipapal prejudice that still lingered in the Nordic countries. He offered a significant reassessment of the person and work of Luther, which paved the way for doctrinal discussion between Catholics and Protestants. And, if nothing else, "it is already a grace that we were able to pray together," as the Pope commented afterward.

Among the fruits of the trip to Scandinavia, I'd like to mention the ecumenical service that was held two years later in Saint Peter's to mark the six hundredth anniversary of the canonization of Saint Brigid of Sweden. On this occasion, the Lutheran primates of Sweden and Finland presided at the first vespers along with John Paul II.

At lunch the same day, one of the two guests asked the Pope whether being flanked by two Lutheran archbishops when he appeared at the altar didn't amount to a recognition of the valid-

ity of their episcopal orders. The Pope answered the joke with
another one: "But couldn't it be the other way around—that by
standing at the altar with me you were recognizing my primacy?"

This is just an example to illustrate the brotherly climate created by the Pope's visit. I noticed the same thing again two years
later when he went to Estonia, which is also a majority Lutheran
country. In the Tallinn cathedral, John Paul II was received as
the "head of the Church." And in his speech, the President
called him "my father" and "Holy Father." There was a unique atmosphere in the cathedral square, which was overflowing with
people. That was real ecumenism for you.

Here's another important episode. The Pope went to Kosice,
Slovakia, to canonize three martyrs who in 1619 had been tor-
tured and killed by the Calvinists in one of a long series of religious wars. The day afterward, though, as he was on his way to
Presov for a meeting with the Greek Catholic community, he
asked Father (today Cardinal) Roberto Tucci (at that time the organizer of the papal trips) to drive him to a monument commemorating the massacre of twenty-four Calvinists at the hands
of Catholics during the same dark period.

This gave the Holy Father a chance to pray at the monument
and even to recite the Our Father with the Lutheran bishop. I
later found out that after the Pope had left, the bishop said,
"I never would have imagined that something like this was possible."

Meanwhile, though, things were starting to change for the worse.
The Anglican Church decided to allow women's ordination,
which added a new area of contention with Catholics. But there
were even more problems on the Orthodox front. Once commu-
nism had ended and the Soviet Empire had broken up, there was

*an explosion of nationalism that unfortunately influenced the
churches, especially the Orthodox, which for long years had
been deprived of freedom and excluded from the process of ecumenism.*

The Holy Father realized right away that the new situation could
complicate Orthodox relations with Rome. Because it was so
united, the Catholic Church had a huge strength, which was
lacking in the Orthodox churches on account of their diversities
and divisions. The Pope thus tried to launch a respectful, tact-
ful, sympathetic dialogue light-years removed from any idea of
proselytism. Unfortunately, though, he didn't always meet with
understanding. His real intentions were not always well understood.

*This was especially the case with the Moscow Partiarchate. One
issue concerned the Eastern Christians united with Rome, who
were demanding restitution of churches and other goods that the
Communist regime had confiscated and transferred to the Orthodox during the era of repression. Another issue emerged when
the Holy See promoted the ecclesiastical jurisdictions in Russia
to the status of actual dioceses. Moscow reacted harshly and
temporarily suspended relations.*

The Holy Father used to say that our churches in Russia, which,
by the way, had just emerged from a period of terrible repression,
had every right to a definitive status. They couldn't be left without pastors.

Besides that, the Moscow Patriarchate had been informed
beforehand. The nuncio had notified them of the Holy See's intention to go ahead with the creation of the four dioceses. More-

over, in order not to offend Orthodox sensibilities, the dioceses were named after their respective cathedrals, and not after their territorial jurisdictions, since the territorial names were already being used by the Orthodox Church.

Maybe they hadn't paid much attention, but at the time the Orthodox agreed, without raising any objections. Only afterward, when they saw the plan actually being implemented, or maybe because they had to deal with internal opposition, did they respond in the way they did. But nobody, and I mean *nobody*, expected a reaction like that!

The result is that nothing ever came of any of the opportunities for a meeting between the Pope and Patriarch Alexei II.

The first missed opportunity came during the papal visit to Hungary in September 1996. The Hungarian government itself, in the person of its ambassador to the Holy See, proposed a meeting in Pannonhalma. But the Holy Synod of the Russian Church opposed the plan.

The second time was in June 1997. The preparations were almost official. Overseeing them on the Catholic side was Archbishop Pierre Duprey, secretary of the Council for Promoting Christian Unity, and on the Orthodox side was Metropolitan Kirill, president of the Department of Foreign Relations. A meeting place was chosen halfway between Rome and Moscow, the Cistercian monastery at Heiligenkreuz, about fifteen miles from Vienna. The location happened to be convenient for Alexei, since he was planning to go to Graz for the Second European Ecumenical Assembly. So everything was ready for the planned June 21 meeting. But at the last minute, Kirill broke the news that it couldn't take place. Once again, the Holy Synod had vetoed the encounter.

The third time was in 2003. The Pope was scheduled to go to Mongolia. This seemed like a good opportunity to make a stop in Kazan, which is in Russian territory, and hand-deliver the icon of Our Lady of Kazan.

The Holy Father ardently wished to make the pilgrimage to Russia as a sign of his determination to contribute to unity among Christians. He also wanted to help clear things up once and for all with the Orthodox Church, which was always very dear to him. This is why he thought it was so important to be able to meet with Alexei II. But the meeting didn't happen this time, either.

In the meantime, the ecumenical scene had quickly darkened. The Orthodox world, obliged to defend Moscow, lined up against Rome and its alleged proselytism.

The Pope refused to give up, though. For starters, he made a spectacular offer in the encyclical *Ut Unum Sint*. He declared that he was ready to dialogue with other Christians in order to work out a new way of exercising the primacy of the Bishop of Rome, so that it could become a cause of unity, rather than continue to be a cause of division. To that end, the Congregation of the Doctrine of the Faith prepared a study on the primacy in the first ten centuries—that is, in the millennium when the Christian world was still united.

Furthermore, in order to reestablish friendly and brotherly relations with the different Orthodox churches, John Paul II undertook, with some risk, a series of trips to places like Romania, where the issue of the Eastern Catholic Church was still unre-

solved; Greece, where the Orthodox bishops hadn't even invited him to come; Moscow's neighbor Ukraine. And yet he was aided by his mea culpas and buoyed up by the conviction that, as he would often put it, the first step was to promote "union in feeling, then union in deed." As a result, the Pope was able to effect a radical change in places and in attitudes that were avowedly hostile before.

I'm still moved when I remember how, during the Holy Father's visit to Bucharest, the people suddenly burst out shouting "*Unitade, unitade*" ("Unity, unity"). Everybody joined in—Orthodox, Catholics, Evangelical Protestants. All of them were shouting for the restoration of the unity that once existed among Christians.

I'd also like to mention his visit to Greece again, because it was a really extraordinary event. During the Holy Father's stay in Athens, we saw the two churches overcome their initial distance and draw closer together by the hour. By the time the Pope left, the Greek Orthodox Church was no longer the same as it was when he had arrived in Greece.

Well, then, how long will we have to wait for the reunion of all Christians? This is a question that even Pope John Paul II asked himself at the end of Ut Unum Sint: "Quanta est nobis via?" How much further do we still have to go? Maybe the six hands that together pushed open the ancient Byzantine door of Saint Paul's were themselves already a first answer. For those hands belonged to Christians who, while still divided, truly wished to come back together again someday.

33.

John Paul II's Jewish Roots

There is an extraordinary continuity between the Wojtyla of the Polish years and Wojtyla as Pope—a continuity in behavior, actions, even words. It is as if his experiences as a young man, and then as a priest and a bishop, had been necessary stages preparing him for the responsibility of the pontificate.

That's right. Think of everything Karol Wojtyla brought with him to Rome—his teaching, his scholarship, his knowledge, his holiness, his way of looking at things, plus his major concerns as a bishop: the family, youth, human rights, doctrinal orthodoxy, the education of the clergy. And I think that all of this, his contribution, we might say, was something he lived out and brought to maturity in the universal horizon that is the papacy's native turf. In the end, he transformed it all into something profoundly new, something that put the stamp of change on his pontificate.

Of all of his experiences in Poland, though, there's probably one that most helps us make sense of what he did afterward on the

*throne of Peter. John Paul II was the first Pope in history to en-
ter a synagogue. Similarly, no other Pope did more to "purify"
Catholic teaching about Judaism, just as no other Pope denounced anti-Semitism more harshly. But this is what we would
expect from a Pope who was born and raised in Wadowice, a
town where living with Jews on a daily basis was the most ordinary thing in the world.*

Wadowice had about ten thousand inhabitants, a third of whom
were Jews. They felt totally Polish and were great patriots. And
in Wadowice, Catholics and Jews lived side by side in peace,
without any conflicts. So, thanks to a daily routine of friendship,
esteem, and tolerance, Karol Wojtyla got to know Judaism from
the inside, which included, of course, in the religious and spiritual sense. His boyhood experience was already leading him to
the conviction that Catholics and Jews are united in their awareness of praying to the same God.

*The Wojtyla family's landlord was Jewish. Karol had Jewish
classmates like Zygmunt and Leopold. He played ball with Jewish friends like Poldek, who was a musician, and no one ever saw
them fighting. Ginka, his slightly older upstairs neighbor, who
first introduced him to the theater, was Jewish. There was also a
Jewish family with whom Karol spent a lot of time: the Klugers.
Most of this time was spent with Jerzy Kluger, one of his closest
friends, whom he had known since elementary school.*

Karol and Jerzy—I should say Lolek and Jurek, as they used to
call each other—were classmates through high school graduation. During that entire period, they would always spend time at

each other's houses. Jurek went to the Wojtylas' because Lolek's father, the former lieutenant, helped him with his homework. Lolek went to Jurek's house to listen to the radio or the musical quartet led by Mr. Kluger, a lawyer who was also president of the local Jewish community. And then Jurek's grandmother, Mrs. Huppert, would often stroll through the main square with the parish priest, Monsignor Prochownik, whereupon they would sit down on a bench and talk so loudly that Ciwek, the only policeman in town, would have to stand guard to keep away the people who would stop to listen.

There you have it: everyday life in Wadowice.

There's a second aspect that explains what we could call the Jewish "roots" of the future Pope. Following the outbreak of World War II, he lived through, though only indirectly, the terrible tragedy euphemistically labeled by its perpetrators as the "final solution," aimed at wiping the Jewish people off the face of the Earth.

After the end of the war, Karol found out that a lot of his Jewish friends had died either on the battlefield or in the Nazi camps. He found out that the Shoah, the extermination of the Jewish people, had been carried out in his own native Poland. And he was so deeply shaken by this terrible experience that it remained forever etched in his memory.

The Kluger family was also annihilated by Hitler's madness. Jurek's mother, his twenty-year-old sister, Tesia, and his grandmother all died in the extermination camps. Jurek himself fought in Italy with General Anders's army. After the end of the war, he

got married and settled in Rome. And it was in Rome that he un-
expectedly ran into his old friend Lolek, who was now arch-
bishop of Kraków.

The friendship was never interrupted, either—not even after the
election to the papacy. Every so often, the Holy Father would invite him and his family to lunch or dinner. And even then they
still addressed each other familiarly, just like they had when they
were classmates. Kluger, now an engineer, treated the Pope as if
he were one of the family, and the Pope really felt like he was one
of the Klugers. He baptized Kluger's daughter (who had converted to Catholicism), then blessed her wedding, and finally
baptized *her* daughter. It was a true, life-long friendship.

We can better understand now why Karol Wojtyla went to
Auschwitz as Pope and said, "I couldn't not come here." And why
he decided to enter a synagogue, the first Pope to do so in two
thousand years, in order to offer a historic gesture of solidarity
with, and reparation toward, all Jews of all times.

In February 1981, the Holy Father made a pastoral visit to the
parish of San Carlo ai Catinari in Rome. And since the old Jewish ghetto was nearby, they organized a meeting between the
Pope and the chief rabbi, Elio Toaff, in the sacristy of the
church. The whole thing was very private, and it didn't last long,
but it was also a first. The ice had already been broken.

Five years later, in February 1986, John Paul II was discussing
a future trip to the United States with his collaborators over
lunch. The archbishop of Los Angeles had suggested that the
Pope visit a synagogue in that city. At that point, someone blurted
out, "Holy Father, then why not begin with your own diocese?"

And so he did, thereby satisfying a wish he himself had long harbored anyway. Archbishop (today Cardinal) Jorge Mejía did an excellent job leading the advance party.

The fact is that it took a Pope like him, who came from a country that had tragically experienced the barbarity of the war and the extermination camps, to repeat the Second Vatican Council's denunciation of the Shoah and of anti-Semitism. These denunciations rang out like an explosion when they were uttered in the synagogue in Rome.

That's right. It took a Pope like him, with a life story like his, to be credible when he recalled the Jewish roots of Christianity, and when he recalled and reaffirmed the unbreakable "spiritual bond" that indissolubly unites Jews and Christians.

It took a Pope like him, who always thought of Catholicism, and lived it out, as the continuation of the Old Testament—yes, it took a Pope like him to pray together with our "older brothers," which was how his faith in and great love for Holy Scripture taught him to call the Jewish people.

As far as the Holy Father was concerned, the visit couldn't have ended any better than with Rabbi Toaff's remark in their private, informal conversation that took place after they had concluded the "official" visit: "We Jews are grateful to you Catholics for bringing the idea of the monotheistic God to the world."

Jews and Christians could finally begin to walk together. Of course, there were also a lot of difficulties, even heated conflicts. The opening of a Carmelite monastery at Auschwitz was one source of controversy. So, too, were Jewish criticisms of the failure—or at least what was judged to be the failure—of certain

Vatican documents to speak out clearly enough about the past, especially about the pontificate of Pius XII and his supposed silence regarding the Holocaust.

But John Paul II always managed to quiet the polemists with a vigorous, authoritative statement. He never forgot to acknowledge that many Christians had been insufficiently robust in their spiritual resistance to Nazism. And he always made a point of reaffirming the irrevocability of God's election of the Jewish people and the uniqueness, or at least the specificity, of the Shoah.

And then, during the Jubilee year, he made a pilgrimage to the Holy Land.

When we entered Yad Vashem, I understood from the emotion on the Holy Father's face why he absolutely wanted to go there. And I think that the emotion he showed was just a tiny part of the emotion he was feeling inside, of the feelings he was sharing with the Jewish people.

Maybe—I say *maybe* because I am just speculating—the Holy Father, feeling the end of his life approaching, was worried that he hadn't done enough to condemn the people and the ideologies responsible for the tragedy of the Holocaust. Perhaps that's why he was so anxiously looking forward to offering a prayer in Yad Vashem in memory of the six million Jews who were killed simply for being Jews—including, horrifyingly, one and a half million children.

Given the weight of this terrible history, the Holy Father surely did the right thing by reducing his words to a minimum and letting silence, the silence of the heart and of memory, do the talking instead.

At that point, Prime Minister Ehud Barak went to the Holy

Father. He seemed to want to show his support and assure the Pope that everyone understood his feelings. He said, "You couldn't have said more than you did."

The next thing I'd like to recall about that visit was another one of the Holy Father's great gestures, which he didn't perform to win over the media, but to express his deep faith. I mean his visit to the Wailing Wall, of course.

In a low voice, the Holy Father repeated the request for forgiveness from the Jewish people that he had already read at Saint Peter's and had brought on a little sheet of paper. When he was finished, he approached the wall and put the paper into one of the chinks.

At the time, I wondered what this scene would mean for Jews. My question was answered a few days later when I read the following statement by Elie Wiesel in a newspaper: "When I was a child, I was always afraid of walking by a church. Now all of that has changed."

34.

Thou Shalt Not Kill in the Name of God

No one said it would be easy to erase, or even just to forget, fourteen centuries of conflict, prejudice, and "holy war" between Christianity and Islam. Since the time of Muhammad, the standard relations between the two religions—with a few rare exceptions—had been governed by a struggle for mutual conquest, if not mutual annihilation. The Christians launched the Crusades, and the Muslims invaded Europe. The Christians put the Cross on their banners, and the Muslims etched the name of Allah on their scimitars and their bullets.

The turning point came with the Second Vatican Council, which took a positive approach to the Muslim religion. Former tensions gradually began to relax. There were joint statements condemning the violence occurring in places like Algeria. But things really changed with the papacy of John Paul II. In fact, La Civiltà Cattolica stated that no other Pope in history showed so much personal "interest" in relations with Muslims.

◆　◆　◆

As you might expect, the experience the Holy Father gained during his trips to Muslim countries played a decisive role in the area of Islamic-Christian relations. The trips deepened his conviction that the Catholic Church should move as quickly as possible to intensify its efforts to enlarge the scope of dialogue and collaboration with Islam. He used to say that the world would also gain from good relations between the two great religious traditions.

In the spring of 1985, the Pope ended a long trip to Africa with a final stop in Morocco. He received an extraordinary welcome for a Pope visiting a Muslim country. King Hassan II took a personal interest in the preparations for the visit, including details such as the arrangement of the altar. The high point, though, was the meeting with at least eighty thousand young Muslims in Casablanca. The crowd in the stadium covered the bleachers and the turf like a shining sea of white. "We must respect, love, and help every human being," John Paul II said with a frankness that won over his audience.

He was forthright about who he was—the Bishop of Rome, the head of the Catholic Church—and about why he had come—to talk about Christ. So he didn't put on any masks or play any games. Above all, though, he spoke as a believer in God to other believers in God. "I would simply like to share with you my witness to what I believe."

It was extraordinary how the young people applauded at all the right moments. It's clear that they couldn't have known what he was going to say or have been coached in any way. So we finally reached the amazing conclusion that they were simply listening with attentive interest to what the Holy Father was telling them. Christians and Muslims are the children of Abraham and believe in one and the same God. They have a lot of things in common both as believers and as men. And today, in our increasingly secular and atheistic world, Christians and Muslims have a special duty to bear common witness to their spiritual values.

It was really an unforgettable meeting. A lot of Arab newspapers reported on it positively, as well.

The following year was the World Day of Prayer for Peace in Assisi. Representatives of Islam—at least of more spiritual, more moderate versions of Islam—also took part. After all, with Islam having more than a billion adherents, it's not surprising that it would include an extreme variety of positions and approaches.

The gathering in Assisi happened to occur at a time when the diversity of opinion among Muslims was becoming increasingly apparent. On the one hand, the conflict between Israel and the Arab world over Palestine was getting worse. On the other hand, integralist groups were triumphing in the field and setting up states governed by Sharia—that is, by the subordination of the civil laws to religious precepts. Another problem was posed by states such as Saudi Arabia, which absolutely forbids Catholic places of worship.

This was a concern that tended to come up more and more frequently whenever the Holy Father would consult with his closest collaborators. He thought the Holy See must do everything in its power to prevent the outbreak of war in the Middle East, especially if it had any semblance of a religious conflict.

Solving problems by armed conflict was simply incompatible with faith in God. It would have been blasphemous to think otherwise. John Paul II's solution was to spread the spirit of Assisi and to promote further dialogue, both among the monotheistic religions and among all religions in general.

John Paul II planned a Jubilee pilgrimage in the footsteps of Abraham, Moses, Jesus, and Paul for the year 2000. He wanted, you might say, to revisit the origins of salvation history in the very places where the living God had left His "footprint."

The first stop was supposed to be Ur of the Chaldees, today part of Iraq, but he was refused the necessary permission. So the Pope had to begin his pilgrimage with a solemn commemoration of Abraham in the Vatican.

He wasn't happy about the negative answer, obviously. The thing that bothered him even more was that they hadn't understood his intention, which was to follow in the footsteps of Abraham, the man whom both Christians and Muslims look up to as their father in faith.

It's odd, though, that they refused him permission to visit Iraq. Cardinal Etchegaray had gone there to arrange the trip. The multinational peacekeepers had already said they could guarantee security. And yet, after a long delay, Saddam Hussein finally said no. He was very courteous about it, of course, and he claimed that he was worried about security risks. But was that the real reason?

And just to make the refusal even more bitter, the Iraqi bishops brought the Pope a brick from Abraham's house during one of their visits to the Vatican. His response was, "You know, I'd always thought Abraham lived in a tent."

◆   ◆   ◆

In spite of that, John Paul II's pilgrimage did give him a chance to walk the paths of the Muslim world. He went to Cairo and to Mount Sinai, as well as to Mount Nebo in Jordan. From there, he journeyed on to Bethlehem, and while in Jerusalem he visited the Dome of the Rock, one of Islam's holiest shrines.

But who could ever have imagined what would happen the following year?

I have to say that as late as three months before the Holy Father's trip to Syria, nothing had been planned or even discussed regarding the Pope's visiting a mosque. No one had ever invited the Pope to enter a Muslim place of worship, either in connection with this trip or in connection with any of the other trips, such as those to Cairo or Jerusalem. I don't know, maybe they were just tactfully trying to spare the Pope embarrassment. And the Pope obviously couldn't invite himself.

Then, out of the blue, the invitation came from Damascus, partly at the suggestion of the Syrian government, partly at the prompting of Muslim groups. In the end, everyone was in agreement, glad to have come up with the idea and glad to have gone through with it.

So on May 6, 2001, John Paul II became the first Pope of the Catholic Church ever to enter a mosque, the Omayyad Mosque in Damascus, where the shrine of John the Baptist is preserved. The visit opened a major chapter in religious history. It wasn't just that it marked a step beyond a troubled past. More important, it signaled a commitment on the part of Christians and Muslims to forswear the abuse of religion as a justification for hatred and violence and to rediscover their common foundations. In short, as the participants said at the time, the visit was a pledge to give the highest-possible profile to the collaboration between the two religions, and not to their opposition, as had all too often been the case in the past.

It looked like it might be the beginning of a period of peaceful and constructive coexistence. The Holy Father made no secret of his hope that the world might attain a certain tranquillity, partly thanks to the spiritual climate created by the Jubilee. He had hopes, then, for a more stable, more widespread peace, as well as for a greater extension of justice.

But then September 11 happened.

Between 8:45 and 9:45 A.M. local time, two airplanes carrying hundreds of passengers slammed into the Twin Towers in New York, while in Washington another crowded plane crashed into the west wing of the Pentagon.

September 11 showed the face of a new terrorism that looked to Al Qaeda and to Osama bin Laden as its head. This new terrorism was invisible, carried out with deadly and sophisticated weapons, funded by billions of dollars, and fed by Islamic fundamentalism. And it had declared war on America and the West—a war that manipulated religion, wreaking death and destruction in the name of God.

The Holy Father was in Castel Gandolfo. The telephone rang. It was Cardinal Sodano, the secretary of state, and he sounded frightened. The Pope indicated that the television should be turned on, and he then saw the dramatic images of the Twin Towers collapsing, with thousands of victims trapped inside. Filled with suffering, he spent the rest of the afternoon going back and forth between the chapel and the television.

The next morning, the Pope celebrated Mass. After the liturgy, he held a special general audience in Saint Peter's Square. I remember that he called it "a dark day in the history of humanity." I also remember that before the prayer, the faithful were asked not to applaud or sing. It was a day of mourning.

He was terribly worried that it wouldn't stop there, that September 11 would trigger an endless spiral of violence. Partly, this was because he thought the spread of the terrorist plague was also due to dire poverty and lack of educational and cultural opportunities in a lot of Arab countries. So he thought that if we were going to defeat terrorism, we also needed to eliminate the huge social and economic inequalities between the First World and the Third.

John Paul II got it right, as in so many other cases. Afghanistan was liberated from the Taliban, but taking out the terrorist bases involved killing hundreds of innocent people. And it very quickly became clear that the war machine could no longer be stopped— or, more precisely, that the men in the driver's seat refused to stop it.

At that point, Pope John Paul II, though bent with age, weariness, and illness, threw himself into what was probably the most painful and exhausting phase in his whole campaign on behalf of peace. He traveled around the world, even visiting far-off places like Azerbaijan, to declare his opposition to violence and "war in the name of God." He sent his envoys to Iraq and the United States, while he himself met with heads of state and politicians, all in an attempt to avert another absurd war—a war for which they'd invented the category "preemptive war," but which would actually be a unilateral and therefore illegal and immoral undertaking.

✦   ✦   ✦

On Saturday, March 15, 2003, the Holy Father, accompanied by Cardinal Sodano and Archishop Tauran, received Cardinal Pio Laghi, who was returning from a mission to the United States. Though he didn't want to throw in the towel, Laghi had a negative answer to relay from the American president. George Bush perfectly understood the Pope's moral arguments, but by that point it was too late to turn back. He had already issued Saddam Hussein an ultimatum that required him to respond within forty-eight hours.

Meanwhile, Cardinal Etchegaray had already come back with the answer of the Iraqi leaders. It wasn't absolutely negative, but it was definitely ambiguous. They were ready to cooperate with UN inspectors, but they weren't forthcoming on the whole issue of so-called weapons of mass destruction.

Since at this point we knew all we needed to know, the Pope used his address at the next day's Angelus to make a sad but firm appeal both to Saddam Hussein and to the countries on the UN Security Council. As he was reading the text from the window, the Holy Father seemed to want to accompany this last hope as it set off into the world. He pled for peace three times: "There is still time to negotiate; there is still room for peace, it is never too late to come to an understanding and to continue discussions."

Apparently, though, he didn't think this was enough. Despite the occasional glimmer of hope, he realized that things were about to deteriorate into open war. He was also afraid that it would become a war of civilizations or, even worse, a "holy war."

So he felt that he had to say what was in his heart and to bear personal testimony. He wanted to remind people that he belonged to a generation of men and women who had known war.

Because of that experience, he felt duty-bound to say "No more war."

Since I was in the study, I saw only his profile. But I could see that his features were drawn and that he was trying to reinforce his words with his right hand.

On the night of March 20, the first bombs began to fall on Baghdad. The second war against Saddam Hussein had begun. John Paul II heard the news early the next morning from the Secretariat of State.

In the days that followed, I saw the Holy Father oppressed by grief. He felt all the enormity of this new tragedy. At the same time, though, I thought he had a certain inward serenity. At no point, not even at the end, did he ever resign himself even to the mere idea of the war. And so he was convinced that it was his duty to do everything he could to stop it. He defended peace, as he had always done.

Whenever some trial was in the offing, he never worried beforehand about whether or not he would be defeated. That simply wasn't an issue for him. The same was true this time. He had tried to do his duty before God, the Church, and man. And he had done it as a free man who wasn't controlled either by the West or by the East—the same as always. Perhaps this is why he was able to use his moral authority and his credibility to keep Islamic-Christian relations from becoming a bone of contention in the war.

At a moment when the world seemed to be exploding under the weight of so many tragic contradictions, he was a solitary witness to peace, someone who reminded us that, in spite of every-

thing, the path of history, the evolution of thought, and, above all, the world's religions tell us that the aspiration to unity is unstoppable. And the words that John Paul II repeated throughout his pontificate—"The world can change"—may be the most valuable legacy he left to twenty-first-century man.

35.

"Let Me Go Home to the Lord"

It's only now, at the end of the story I've tried to tell about my forty years at Karol Wojtyla's side, that I realize I've completely skipped over the account of the Holy Father's illness and suffering.

I need to talk about this aspect of his life, though. For—and I am not exaggerating for effect—it was one long martyrdom from start to finish. John Paul II suffered terribly in his body. But he also suffered in his spirit when bodily afflictions forced him to cut back on, or even to suspend, activities that were part of his mission as universal shepherd. Cardinal Ratzinger, who would succeed him as Pope, put it like this: "In his life, the word *cross* is not just a word."

That said, Karol Wojtyla had learned to accept suffering as a part of human existence and thus to live with pain and sickness, which is probably the reason why I haven't spoken of this part of his life until now. The main key to his ability to say yes in such circumstances was his spirituality and the personal relationship he had built with God. "I wish to follow Him" were the opening words of his will. And because his basic choice was to follow the Lord, he understood that life is a gift that has to be lived fully to the end. That's why he was able to accept everything God willed for his life.

You have to remember, too, that he was already familiar with suffering as a boy. He was still quite young when he lost both his parents and his brother. He was struck by a German truck and seriously hurt. He also suffered under totalitarianism: first under Nazism and then under the Communist regime. Certainly his suffering under communism wasn't made any easier by all of his responsibilities as a bishop.

Don't forget the assassination attempt, either. After he was shot, he endured agonizing bodily suffering, and at one point was even at death's door. But that wasn't the only pain he felt. He was also spiritually wounded to the core. Why had another man tried to kill him?

I remember that when he left Gemelli, he said that he thanked God not only for saving his life but also for allowing him to join the community of the sick who were suffering in the hospital. Do you see what I mean? Lying in the hospital, he really felt like one of the sick; he really suffered, in part because his suffering united him with other people in the same condition. And this experience led the Holy Father to write the apostolic letter *Salvifici Doloris,* where he explains the deep meaning of suffering. If it's lived out in union with Christ crucified and risen, suffering acquires an immense value on the level of faith and yields spiritual benefits for the Church and the world.

He said as much on the very opening day of his pontificate, when he asked that space be reserved in the first row so that the sick could participate in the installation ceremony. But after his hospitalization, he sent the message even more frequently.

Whenever he would visit a parish or go on one of his trips, he would make an appointment to meet with the sick, the suffering, and the handicapped. He went to San Francisco and took an AIDS-infected baby in his arms. He visited a leper colony in Korea and kissed one of the inmates. These sorts of gestures were intended to remind those who suffer—not to mention our egotistical world—of the value suffering has in God's eyes when it is lived in union with Chirst. The Pope wanted to remind people that accepting suffering doesn't mean losing their dignity.

So the Holy Father endured physical pain and illness with great serenity and patience—indeed, I'd have to say, with great Christian manliness. And meanwhile, he went on doggedly fulfilling his mission. But the thing that struck me most was that he never burdened others with his physical ailments. He never burdened those of us who were living with him. And he never burdened "outsiders," for example the people he visited on his travels. So much so, in fact, that I think a lot of people hardly knew that he had any physical ailments at all.

Of course, he didn't shy away from talking about his sufferings in public. Do you remember when, at an Angelus address in June 1992, he confided to the faithful in Saint Peter's Square that he was checking into Gemelli that evening for some medical tests? Think about it: a Pope who (without going into the details) informed the faithful that he was going to have an intestinal tumor removed. And not only did he not hide his illnesses; he even made a joke out of them. For example, once, after several trips to Gemelli, he started calling the hospital "Vatican III."

You see, that was Karol Wojtyla, both as a human being and as a man of the spirit. And though he increasingly looked the part of an invalid, he remained in character, even when he began to be ravaged by illness. Even when this man who had once walked the highways and byways of the world was confined to a wheel-chair. Even when his voice, which had once rung out everywhere with the message of Vatican II, began to grow so faint and labored that soon he could no longer even speak or swallow. Even when his gaze, which had once penetrated your soul and made you feel like the sole object of his attention, was hidden under a daily more rigid and expressionless mask.

Without even realizing it, I'm already talking about the end, or the prelude to the end. But I have to remind you that he first began to show symptoms of his terrible illness as early as 1991, when some of the fingers of his left hand started to shake. Then, in 1993, when he slipped and fell, dislocating his right shoulder, Dr. Buzzonetti became convinced that the fall was partly due to an impaired sense of balance, which indicated an extrapyramidal neurological syndrome: Parkinson's disease.

I have to say that when the doctor told me the news, I understood how serious the matter was, but, going on what I knew about Parkinson's, I tried to focus on the positives. For example, I knew that while the disease couldn't be completely reversed, it could at least be slowed down significantly if caught in time. Plus, when Buzzonetti informed the Holy Father, he, the Pope, didn't seem particularly upset. He merely asked a few questions. He assured the doctor that he was willing to be treated, but he also wanted to be allowed to continue carrying out his mission.

This may be one of the reasons why it wasn't thought necessary to inform the public about the disease right away, especially since the Pope continued to go about his work as normal.

As the months and years went by, though, the disease began to take a visible toll on the Holy Father's body and to diminish his physical capabilities. This obviously started to impair the exercise of his pastoral ministry and, above all, to limit his travels. He had already made his peace with the idea of slowing things down and cutting back on the number of engagements. But as time went on, he also had to rely on being transported by other people. This was occurring with increasing frequency, too, though at first this was mainly because of an ankle operation, not because of the Parkinson's per se. Having to be carried was the thing that bothered him the most; you could tell by certain signs of impatience. He regarded the lack of autonomous movement as an obstacle to his direct, immediate relationship with people.

At the time, various newspapers were criticizing the so-called display of the Pope's suffering. They said that a man in his condition should have canceled his public appearances and kept more to the Vatican. Those criticisms were much more hurtful to me and others close to John Paul II than they were to the Holy Father himself. He didn't pay any attention to such talk. I've already explained that he had commissioned a study of the issue of resignation and made the decision to continue with his mission as long as the Lord gave him the necessary strength.

Meanwhile, he was preparing himself for the big step. In fact, you'd have to say that he had been preparing himself for a long time. You can tell just by reading his will. He started writing it during a retreat in 1979, just a few months after his election, and he continued to update it during annual retreats until the year 2000. The process of updating the will was an examination of conscience, a chance for him to square things with himself. Most important, though, it was a chance for him to reaffirm his readiness to appear before the Lord and return the gift of life the Lord had given him. John Paul II felt this readiness with calm and total conviction.

So he had never been afraid of death, and he wasn't afraid of it now, though he could already glimpse the door that would open to his final meeting with God. He liked to be taken to the chapel, where he would spend a long time speaking with the Lord. And when you watched him pray, you understood exactly what Paul meant when he talked about enduring suffering in order to make up what is lacking to the sufferings of Christ for the sake of Christ's body, the Church.

Toward the end of January 2005, John Paul II fell ill again. It happened during the Angelus address on the last Sunday of the month. He had trouble speaking and his voice was hoarse. It seemed to be a simple flu, but within a few hours it got worse. The doctors explained that it was an acute laryngotracheitis aggravated by a laryngospasm. At dinner on the evening of February 1, the Holy Father was having trouble breathing. We tried to help him, but the shortness of breath wouldn't go away. So we had to check him into Gemelli.

He recovered very quickly. February 9 was the first day of Lent. He concelebrated the Eucharist and blessed the ashes. It was supposed to be a moment of contrition and repentance, but when I went to put the ashes on his forehead and saw how well he was recovering, I felt extremely happy. The following day, he went back home.

Unfortunately, he had a relapse soon after that. The Holy Father was having increasing trouble breathing day and night. It was especially hard for him to inhale. His breath made a hollow, rattling noise. The evening of February 23 was dramatic. At dinner, the Pope's body was convulsed by a new crisis; he was almost asphyxiating. One of the guests, an old friend of his, Cardinal Marian Jaworski, the Latin-rite archbishop of Lviv, was so taken aback that he immediately decided to give the sacrament of anointing to "his" Karol. The situation deteriorated during the night, and so the next day we decided to check the Pope into Gemelli again.

But medical treatment wasn't enough. It was no longer working. Buzzonetti conferred with his colleagues and came back with the recommendation of a tracheotomy. He said it was urgently needed to ensure ease of breathing and to avoid a new, and worse, episode of suffocation. When they told the Holy Father, he turned to me and, speaking into one ear, said I should ask the doctors whether it wouldn't be possible to postpone the surgery until his summer vacation. But when he saw the general reaction, he immediately gave his consent. Once again, he showed his sense of humor. When Buzzonetti tried to reassure him—"Your Holiness, it will be a simple operation"—the Pope quipped, "Simple for whom?"

Of course they told him before going in that he would be unable to speak for a certain period of time. It was only afterward, though, when he woke up from the anesthesia, that he concretely realized what that meant. He signed to me that he wanted to write something. I found him a sheet of paper and a pen. With a somewhat shaky hand, he tossed off a few words: "What have they done to me?! But . . . *totus tuus.*" He was trying to express both all the regret he felt at no longer being able to speak and his resolute, total self-abandonment into Our Lady's hands.

John Paul II was now back in the Vatican, but for the first time since the beginning of his pontificate he was unable to lead the celebration of the Paschal Triduum. On Good Friday, though, he did watch the Via Crucis in the Colosseum on a TV screen set up in his private chapel. At the fourteenth station, he clasped the crucifix, as if to unite himself to Christ and to join his suffering to that of the Son of God, who had died on the Cross.

I felt that the moment was arriving; the Lord was calling him.

The Holy Father at least wanted to give the Easter Sunday "Urbi et Orbi" blessing. He had carefully prepared himself, rehearsing just before the ceremony. Everything seemed to be all right. But then, when Cardinal Sodano had finished reading his address in Saint Peter's Square, the Pope stood motionless at the window, as if frozen. He must have been overwhelmed by a combination of emotion and pain. In any case, he couldn't give the blessing. He whispered, "My voice is gone." Then, still silent, he made the sign of the cross three times, waved to the crowd, and gestured that he wanted to withdraw.

He was deeply shaken and saddened. He also seemed exhausted by his unsuccessful attempt to speak. The people in the square were full of emotion; they were applauding him and calling out his name, but he felt the whole weight of the powerlessness and suffering he had displayed. He looked into my eyes and said, "Maybe it would be better for me to die if I can't fulfill the mission that has been entrusted to me." Before I could answer, he added, "Thy will be done. . . . *Totus tuus.*" He wasn't expressing desperation, but submission to God's will.

On Wednesday, March, 30, the Pope appeared at his window again to greet five thousand kids who had come from the archdiocese of Milan for the profession of faith. We thought—me especially—that he should limit himself to blessing the group. But after giving the blessing, he very decisively waved the microphone closer. He wanted to say something, even if it was just a word, to thank the kids. But no sound came out of his mouth.

As he came away from the window, he didn't even show the impatience that he had displayed at Easter. By this point, he knew. He was ready.

The next day at around 11:00 A.M. he was in the chapel celebrating Mass. All of a sudden, his body was jolted as if something had exploded inside him. He had a high fever—almost 104 degrees. The doctors immediately diagnosed the problem: He had suffered a severe septic shock and a collapse of the cardiovascular system. The cause: a urinary tract infection. There would be no hospitalization this time, though. I reminded Dr. Buzzonetti of the Pope's firm intention not to go back to the hospital. He meant to suffer and die at home, near the tomb of Peter. And he could receive the indispensable medical care just as easily at home as in the hospital.

So now, John Paul II was in his room. On the wall facing the bed, there was a picture of the suffering Christ bound with cords and an image of Our Lady of Czestochowa. On the nightstand, he had a picture of his parents. We celebrated Mass there, and when the service was over, we went up one by one to kiss his hand. When it was my turn, he stroked my head and said, "Stasiu." Next came the sisters in charge of the house, each of whom he addressed personally. The doctors and the nurses came up last.

That Friday was a day of prayer: Mass, the Way of the Cross, Terce, and some Scripture passages read by a great friend of Karol Wojtyla's, Tadeusz Styczeń. The Pope's general condition was extremely serious. At this point, he could say only a few syllables, and even that was difficult.

And so we come to Saturday, April 2.

I would like to be able to remember absolutely everything.

There was an atmosphere of great serenity in the room. The

Holy Father blessed the crowns that would be placed on the image of Our Lady of Czestochowa in the Vatican Grotto, plus two others that would be sent to Jasna Góra. Then he bid farewell to his closest collaborators: cardinals, bishops from the Secretariat of State, directors of various Vatican offices. He also wanted to say good-bye to Francesco, who was in charge of cleaning the papal apartments.

Although he obviously had trouble expressing himself, he was still fully conscious, because he asked us to read the Gospel of Saint John out loud. It wasn't our idea, but his. Even on the day he died, he wanted to do what he had done his whole life: feed on Holy Scripture.

Father Styczeń began to read John chapter by chapter. He read nine chapters in all. The book still has a mark indicating where he finished reading. For it was at that moment that the Holy Father's life on Earth came to a close.

So, you, see, in his very last moments, the Holy Father went back to being what he basically had always been: a man of prayer. He was a man of God, a man who lived in intimate communion with God. Prayer was thus the constant foundation of his life. When he had to meet with someone, make an important decision, write a document, or go on a journey, he always turned to God first. The first thing he would do was pray.

He did the same thing on the day when he made his last, great voyage. Before setting out, he recited all his daily prayers (with the help of those who were watching with him); during exposition of the Blessed Sacrament he had meditated and even prayed the Office of Readings for Sunday.

At a certain point, Sister Tobiana felt him looking at her. She put her ear up to his mouth. With a weak, almost inaudible voice, he said, "Let me go home to the Lord." The nun ran out of the room. She tried to tell us what had happened, but she couldn't stop crying.

I only thought of it later, but it's extraordinary that he spoke his last words to a woman.

Around seven o'clock that evening, the Holy Father fell into a coma. The only light in the room came from a small candle that he himself had blessed on February 2 for the Feast of the Presentation.

A crowd had been gathering in Saint Peter's Square and the adjacent streets. More and more people, especially young people, kept coming. You could hear them shouting, *"Giovanni Paolo! Viva il Papa"* all the way from the fourth floor. I'm convinced that he heard them. How could he not have?

It was almost 9:00 P.M. when I suddenly felt a kind of imperious command inside me: I had to celebrate Mass. So I started concelebrating with Cardinal Jaworski, Archbishop Rylko, and two Polish priests, Styczeń and Mokrzycki. It was the vigil Mass for Divine Mercy Sunday, a solemnity that was dear to the Pope. The Gospel, too, was from John: "Jesus came and stood in their midst and said, 'Peace be with you.'" At Communion, I was able to give him a few drops of the precious blood of Christ as viaticum.

It was 9:37 P.M. We had already noticed that the Holy Father was no longer breathing. But it was only at that precise moment that we looked at the monitor and saw that his great heart, which had kept beating for a few more seconds, had finally stopped.

Dr. Buzzonetti bent over him. He raised his eyes a little and whispered, "He's gone home to the Lord."

Meanwhile, someone had stopped the hands of the clock at the precise time of the Pope's death.

And, as if we had all agreed beforehand, we started to sing the

Te Deum. Not the Requiem, because we weren't mourning, but the Te Deum, because we wanted to thank God for the gift he had given us, the gift of the person of the Holy Father, of Karol Wojtyla.

We were crying, of course. How could we have not cried? We were crying tears of grief and joy at the same time. And at that point, they turned on all the lights in the house.

I don't remember anything else after that. It's as if darkness suddenly descended on me and in me. I knew perfectly well what had happened, but *afterward* it was as if I couldn't accept it. Or couldn't understand it. I put myself in the Lord's hands, but whenever I thought my heart was at peace, the darkness would suddenly fall again.

Until it was time to say farewell.

There were immense crowds at the entombment, as everyone knows. A lot of important people had come from far away to be there. But, more important, his people were there. Thousands of the young people he had loved were there. There were a lot of the placards we've all seen: *"Santo subito"* (sainthood now!). Those impatient words said it all. Saint Peter's Square was all lit up. And so was my heart.

At the end of his homily, Cardinal Ratzinger pointed to the window and said that John Paul II was surely there watching and blessing us. I turned around, too. I couldn't not turn around. But looking up would have been too much for me.

At the end, when they came to the portico of the basilica, the pallbearers slowly turned the coffin around. It was as if they wanted to give him one last chance to look out on the square and bid his final farewell to the world and its inhabitants.

But was it his final farewell to me, too?

No, I don't think so. At that moment, I wasn't thinking of myself. I was just living the moment with everyone else. And everyone was shaken and upset. For me, though, it was an unforgettable event.

Meanwhile, the procession was filing into the basilica. It was time to take the bier down to the tomb.

And just then, I had a thought.

I had accompanied him for almost forty years: twelve in Kraków and then twenty-seven in Rome. I was always with him, always at his side.

Now, in the moment of death, he'd gone on alone.

I had accompanied him to a certain point, but then he'd gone on alone from there. And the fact that this time I wasn't able to accompany him hit me like a ton of bricks.

Of course he hasn't left us. We feel his presence, and we experience all the many graces obtained by his intercession. And of course I did accompany him through an important stage of the Church's journey.

But now he's gone on alone.

And now? Who is accompanying him on the other side?

3/08

LEWES PUBLIC LIBRARY, INC.
111 ADAMS AVENUE
LEWES, DE 19958
(302) 645-4633